Grandads Grandmas Nanas & Poppas

A Celebration of New Zealand Families

Photography by Terry Winn

Text by Karen Holdom

Hodder Moa Beckett

ISBN 1-86958-757-X

Published in 1999 by Hodder Moa Beckett Publishers Limited, [a member of the Hodder Headline Group]; 4 Whetu Place, Mairangi Bay, Auckland, New Zealand

Produced and designed by Hodder Moa Beckett Publishers Ltd
Film by Microdot, Auckland
Printed by South China Printing Co., Hong Kong

Dedications & Acknowledgements

It has been my privilege to meet all the grandparents and their grandchildren featured in this book, and to experience the special relationships that they share. Special thanks to Vicki, my wife, business partner and best friend, for sharing my dreams and aspirations.
To my studio team, Helen and Mark, thank you for your loyalty and co-operation, and many thanks to all the mums and dads who organised, transported and encouraged their families to be involved.
A special dedication goes to both Sol Filler and Lesley Ford.
In memory of two wonderful people of great courage.

Terry Winn

A special dedication to my grandparents, Betty and Tom,
Manu and Frank.

Karen Holdom

Contents

Introduction

When photographer Terry Winn first photographed 99-year-old Ben (pictured right), he didn't expect that it would lead to a book. Yet the portrait of Ben sparked an idea and in February and March of 1998, Terry advertised for grandparents and grandchildren who were willing to have their portraits taken for a book about grandparents. One thing led to another and, with a publisher keen on the project and journalist Karen Holdom on board to write the stories, the project was under way.

In *Grandads, Grandmas, Nanas & Poppas*, people open their hearts about the precious relationship between young and old. The book takes us into the living rooms and back gardens of some of New Zealand's most famous families: Paul Reeves camps in the backyard with his granddaughter; Alison Holst makes finger puppets with her granddaughter Elizabeth; Colin Meads cooks a hearty farm breakfast for his tribe of 11 grandchildren; artist Sylvia Siddell paints a portrait of her grandson Max as Alexander the Great; and former All Black Bull Allen tells his grandfather why he shaved his head.

The book captures a moment in time of the New Zealand family. Grandparents from all over the country are featured and, different though they are, the one thing they have in common is they all adore their grandchildren. There are grandparents from the city and the country and from different ages, cultural groups and religions.

Many have thought deeply about the role they want to play in their grandchildren's lives – especially those who've had health scares or been through difficult times that have made them aware that they won't always be there to share their grandchildren's lives. Often grandparents find they have more time to spend with their grandchildren than they did with their own kids and can enjoy the relationship without the responsibility of being a parent.

Grandchildren, too, think that the bond is different and say they tell their grandparents things that they wouldn't necessarily share with their parents. As grandchildren grow into adolescence and become more independent, the relationship changes and sometimes the intensity of the bond weakens, becoming stronger again later in life as with Jane Dent and her grandmother Vi Donaldson who love discussing sport together.

Grandparents are often the ones who pass on family stories and traditions that have shaped the lives of their family in profound ways. These stories unfold against the backdrop of history and, reading them, you realise how events that occurred on the other side of the world in past decades have shaped the lives of New Zealanders today, making us an increasingly diverse, multicultural country.

Perhaps that's why people who have surviving grandparents are blessed – they know where they've come from and the events that have shaped them.

Dignified grandmother Fanny Sew Hoy tells how, pregnant with her sixth child, she fled the Japanese invasion of Southern China in 1938 before being reunited with her husband in New Zealand nine years later. Jewish grandfather Sol Filler told why it was important that his grandchildren remembered him for his jokes as well as his years of suffering at the hands of the Nazis during the Holocaust. (Sol Filler passed away during the production of this book.)

As well as stories, grandparents hand down their skills – eminent Maori weaver Diggeress Te Kanawa teaches her granddaughter Clowdy to weave a korowai [feather cloak] while master carver Tuti Tukaokao plans to teach his granddaughter Rita-Kay to carve when she is old enough, breaking what was once the cardinal rule that women must not carve.

This book shatters stereotypes of grandparents as cosy individuals bottling jam and pruning roses and shows us a dynamic, varied group of people all with their own take on what it means to be a grandparent. Likewise, the grandchildren in the book are not always sweet, well-behaved kids playing on the swing in the backyard.

There are rich stories here – the ordinary triumphs and tragedies that make up New Zealand family life – as well as stories of courage and humour. Meet fiery grandmother Kerewai Conrad who catches trevally on a handline in the Far North and who strenuously resists her family's attempts to stop her driving, almost running them over in the process. Meet quiet Maniototo farmer and poet Ross McMillan who's watching thunderclouds in the sky and waiting for a break in the region's worst drought in living memory.

What's fascinating in *Grandads, Grandmas, Nanas & Poppas* is how the definition of "family" in New Zealand has changed. With more open adoption laws it's now possible for a child to have several grandmothers, as does Gamel O'Brien of Oamaru, whose three grandmothers all live in the same town and meet at the same pub on Friday nights. It is also possible for a grandfather to take on the role of parent. Kaumatua Piripi Cope's grandson Tamahou fretted so much when separated from him as a baby that his parents decided to allow Piripi to adopt him.

Family traditions are changing as people become more mobile and have access to more opportunities. This is obvious in the rural families interviewed for the book. Though Maniototo farmer Jim Becker would love his grandsons to stay on the family farm, he knows they will travel and take other career options open to them.

The interviews in this book are heartwarming and candid. In their own way, all the grandparents interviewed are extraordinary and, no matter who they are or where they're from, they all love and cherish their grandchildren.

Dame Pat Evison & her grandchildren

Long before she became a Dame, Pat Evison daydreamed about the kind of grandmother she would be. She'd missed out on having grandparents of her own and looked forward to being a guiding influence in her grandchildren's lives.

But geography intervened and, with seven granddaughters and one grandson spread around the globe, Wellington-based Dame Patricia, known to her grandchildren as Minga, has to be content with doing the job long distance most of the time.

"I didn't have any grandparents myself," she says. "They were dead before I was born and I've always felt greatly deprived because I think grandparents should be important in your life. I would have liked to have been a very good grandmother."

Dame Patricia, 75, has four grandchildren in France, to her daughter Anne; two in Canada, to son John; and two in Christchurch, to son Tim.

As well as the sheer distance between her and the children, Dame Patricia's physical disabilities also place barriers between her and the children when they do meet. She's losing her sight, as a result of diabetes-related damage to her eyes, and suffers painful osteoarthritis in one knee, which makes it impossible to be on her feet too long or to travel over uneven ground. She can't take part in activities like skiing with her French grandchildren, which her husband Roger still loves to do.

"I'm physically restricted and I always feel that there are so many wonderful things that they should be doing that I can't share, and I don't want to be a drag on the situation.

"For instance, the family is coming back to New Zealand for the ski season, but I won't see very much of them because they'll be in the Craigieburn Valley Skifield, and it's very difficult to get to the accommodation."

Dame Patricia says the three sets of grandchildren are all very different, something she puts down to a combination of personality and culture.

She says the Canadian grandchildren, Letitia and Rhiannon, are "lovely looking girls with pleasant natures", who went out of their way to help her develop her non-

existent computer skills when she was last in Canada, starting to write her autobiography.

"My son John borrowed a 20-inch screen and discovered that, with a dark blue background and white letters, I could actually see what I was writing. There were so many things that I didn't understand about computers. I was totally ignorant. So I would call, 'Cry for help!' There were four computer-wise people in the house and one would come running. The girls were really helpful and patient."

But Dame Patricia is concerned that Letitia, 17, and Rhiannon, 16, show a lack of interest in books – something she fails to understand, having had a passion for the written word since she was a small child.

"What intrigued me was the time they spent in front of the television. Something was on – I think the Olympic Games. Their lives had somehow been taken over by music, the computer or the television or sport – they play a lot of sport."

Dame Patricia shared her feelings with the girls' parents but didn't labour the point. "I don't stress it, but I would like to because one of the saddest things to me now is that I can't read. I feel awfully deprived by this and if I'm on my own in the house, I have to either listen to the radio, or watch the TV without really seeing what I'm watching. But talking books are great."

The four grandchildren in France, Timothee, Madeline, Beatrice and Clementine, share her love of books and also seem to have inherited some of the genes which made Dame Patricia an icon of the stage and small screen. "They are lovely kids – artistic, creative and they performed the most wonderful *spectacles*! They would spend a whole afternoon preparing the entertainment for the grown-ups at night. They wrote their own entertainment, chose their own music, made their own scenery – I loved it."

However, Dame Patricia has reservations about the challenges her French–New Zealand grandchildren face being raised in a bicultural household. "They have had six years in Rotorua and they sound exactly like children who have been brought up there. Now they're back in France wondering what has struck them!"

She says the French education system is tough for children, and she feels for the youngsters who've left behind their friends and New Zealand life to live in a vastly different culture.

Dame Patricia's two youngest grandchildren, Abbey-Rose, four, and Maisie-Ella, one, live in Christchurch.

They are too young for her to be sure of their personalities, but she's already delighted at their love of books.

"They are absolutely potty about books. We took the elder one to the doctor, and in the waiting room there was a basket of toys and a basket of books. I went to pick up the basket of toys and Abbey-Rose went immediately to pick up the basket of books. She will spend hours reading books. That's very good."

So far Dame Patricia's time with the two girls has been limited to when the whole family visits or she heads to Christchurch, but she's hoping eventually the girls will come on their own for holidays.

"We tried to persuade Tim to let Abbey-Rose come up for a while, but he feels she's too young. Also, because I'm a bit decrepit and she's quick on her feet, I think they feel she would get away from me and go crossing roads on her own or something!"

Time spent with the girls usually revolves around story telling – something Dame Patricia delights in doing even without the benefit of books. "Maisie is a bit little, but Abbey-Rose loves stories of Goldilocks or anything at all, so I will tell her in my own words, and I always make up a few things that are different, which is always a good idea."

She says Abbey-Rose is an artist. "Abbey-Rose is absolutely splendid at painting. I have a wonderful painting on my wall she did before she was two on a piece of canvas that her mother Sally gave her. She's actually won colouring-in competitions in the newspaper and won a family ticket to a play at the Court Theatre, and another time a family ticket to the Antarctic Centre. She's worth her weight in gold. A gifted child."

Dame Patricia has thought long and hard about the legacy she wants to leave her grandchildren.

"I've thought about writing a letter, a grandmotherly letter, to them all – not aiming it to any one of them specifically. There always seem to be two sorts of people in the world, givers and takers. To me, the givers in life have always been the happiest and the takers have usually been the ones with a pout, or the mouth turned down because they can't get what they want to take, or they can't take it without an argument.

"I personally have had such a happy life that I would love to see the kids developing the values in life that I think bring happiness, and one of those is consideration for other people and other people's things. My mother taught me that if you are given the opportunity to stay in somebody else's house you always left it cleaner and tidier than when you went in."

What will her grandchildren remember of her? "That I thought my family was important, really because I think that that is important. It's so lovely to see the cousins playing together. That is a great joy."

Dame Patricia is hopeful she'll be seeing a lot more of that – even long after she's dead and gone. "They better have their eyes in the back of their heads because I will have my eyes wherever they are!"

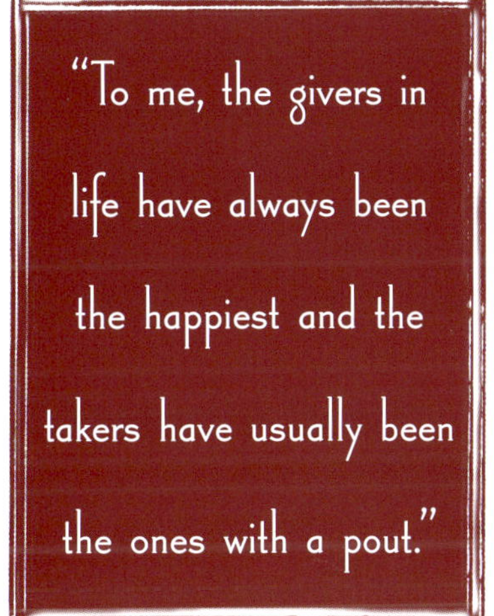

Kerewai Conrad & her granddaughter Rosie

osie Conrad's cheerful face distorts in mock horror as she recalls childhood memories of her grandmother. "What was she like?" she asks, wide-eyed. "She was evil! Dad was 44 when he died and she gave him his last hiding at 38 – with a broomstick!"

Rosie's sister Leisha pipes up, "When you look at how frail Nanny is you would never think in a million years she would do the things she did, but she was one of the meanest grandmothers. If we were late home from school she used to stand on the end of the driveway with a piece of alkathene pipe and give us a whack!"

Rosie cautions her sister to stop, "If she reads this she'll kill us!"

The pair collapse into laughter again before racking their memories for more outrageous stories about their 77-year-old grandmother Kerewai Conrad. Their courage lies in the fact they're sitting in the safety of Leisha's living room in Auckland, 400 km from Rosie's Far North home and the wrath of Kerewai next door.

Of course Kerewai thinks it's hilarious that her grandchildren should be scared of her.

"Ha ha, it's because I have a big mouth," she laughs, without a hint of apology. "We have lots of fruit trees and grandchildren are real little devils. You see them hanging up in the tree – one of them got caught up on top of one once. I get hold of my walking stick and hammer them with it."

Does she like being a grandmother? "I get ho ha with it sometimes," she grumbles. "The only time I like them is when they say, 'Oh Nanny, I sent you some money in the envelope.'" She bursts into laughter again.

Mind you, considering the number of grandchildren she has, who could blame her for getting a little impatient? Kerewai and her husband Niki, who died in 1987, had 13 children and, at last count, 23 grandchildren – seven of whom she raised herself with another five who weren't strictly grandchildren, but were treated as such. To date there are 20 great-grandchildren, including Rosie's daughters Kodie, five, and Tamala, three months.

Rosie, 29, readily acknowledges the sheer size of Kerewai's household meant she had to be tough. "There were always heaps of kids, heaps of work to do. She

always had a garden and went netting for fish – well she had to. She had to feed the troops."

Kerewai, of the tribes Te Rarawa and Te Aupouri, was raised at Whangape, south of Kaitaia, but moved to Te Kao, one of New Zealand's northern-most settlements, when she married Niki Conrad at 21. She's lived in "the bottom house" of the family farm at Te Kao as long as Rosie (who grew up and still lives in "the top house") can remember.

"Nanny has always been there," she says. "Everything revolved around kai the whole time. Nanny always fed everyone who came to her house, always different people. She was hard. She's eased now because she's older, but when she was young she had to be, because there were so many people there."

Kerewai knew all about self-sufficiency, how to grow and catch food, to live on a tight budget and come up with ingenious ways to make money.

"Nanny and Mum taught us to weave and we used to make flax kits and bring them all the way down to Auckland, and a guy in Queen Street would pay $5 for them. That was our pocket money," she recalls.

"We used to sit in our shed and be weaving and see all our mates going out on their horses when we had to stay and make some money. But it was good in the end because when we got our money back we would go and buy us things like push bikes they could never afford."

Over the years, led by their grandmother and mother Bonnie, they took on other schemes such as smoking fish and selling it, picking lupin seed and even seaweed. "There's money there to be made," says Rosie. "You just have to know how to make it. Over the years the things Nanny and Mum have taught us have become family traditions and I think our kids will do them too."

Apart from a few years in Auckland and Australia, Rosie has lived in Te Kao all her life, returning as a young adult in 1993, three years after her dad, Bullu, died, to work on the family farm.

"I would rather bring up my kids at Te Kao because they value things more," says Rosie. "Whatever my girl Kodie has she treasures, whereas in Auckland it's 'Oh if that one breaks I'll go and get a new one.' Up here you can't do that – our closest town is an hour away. It's a better life up here."

Kerewai is pleased those values have been picked up. "That's how they live now. I taught them how to do it. Most of them work for their money and sell things for themselves."

Traditions are important to Kerewai, and her grandchildren have learned from that. "It's just little things," says Rosie, "old Maori ways that Nanny does that other people don't do any more. Like when men are sitting on the floor, women are not supposed to step over their legs; things like that that people forget."

Kerewai and her late husband are well-known figures in the north. Niki was a member of the New Zealand Maori Council and many committees governing Maori affairs. Whenever dignitaries visited the Far North, the

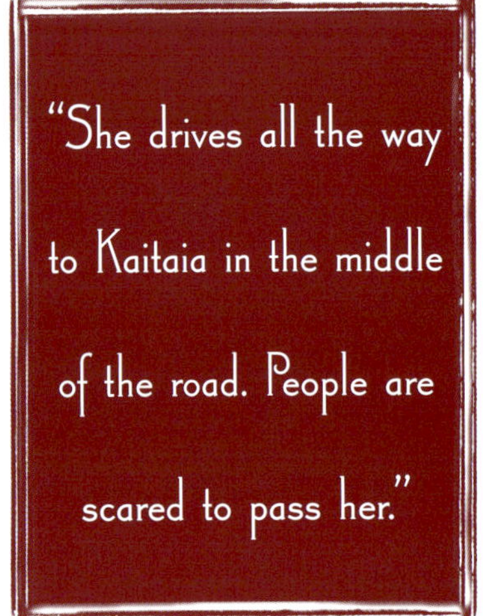

Conrad house was a stopping point and for many years Niki was the chief of the big Ngatoki waka at Waitangi celebrations, while Kerewai was and still is the chief cook.

Another thing Kerewai Conrad is famous for is her driving. "We've had her tested and her eyes are fine, everything is fine, but it's her reaction time. She's been through five cars!" wails Rosie, leaning forward, mimicking her grandmother peering over the wheel at the road ahead. "She drives all the way to Kaitaia in the middle of the road. People are scared to pass her. Most people slow down for the corners, but Nanny gives it the guts. 'It's so my car won't skid,' she says."

Kerewai scoffs. "Don't talk about that driving!" she says with a laugh. "I have a Hillman and they always say to me, 'Nanny you better stop driving' and I say, 'Well if the traffic cop is giving me a licence with my own money, I'm my own boss so shut up.' I get around. I drive to Kaitaia and I get to Whangarei no problem."

Rosie rolls her eyes at the thought. "The other night I was sitting at my house and I heard someone yelling. It was pouring with rain and she had driven back from church – she's a Seventh Day Adventist – and missed the driveway and ended up in the drain. It's never her fault. She ran a guy off the Herekino Gorge. It wasn't her fault. She was coming up the Awanui straight and she reckons she was hit by a bit of sun strike, so she rammed up the back of a Department of Conservation truck! She is still paying them off to this day!

"You can't stop her. You take the keys out of the car, she gets the spare set. You take the battery out, she gets another battery," says Rosie. "One time Nanny hopped in her car ready to go to town and we said, 'No, it's a bit far for an old lady' and my brother reached in to grab the keys so she put her foot on the gas and near ran him over. He flew back and she's gone! She's off up the road! You can't catch her."

While Kerewai appears tough, her grandchildren are well aware that underneath the hard shell there is a lot of pain.

"I remember when my dad died we were at Nan's house and Nanny was looking out her bedroom window, and I used to think she was so mean because she never cried when my dad died," says Leisha. "I went out to some other old people and said, 'How come Nan can't cry?' and they said, 'Your grandmother has lived through the death of four of her children and has seen her grandchildren pass. She must be hurting inside, but she's a tough person. She holds a lot of emotion in.'"

Rosie nods. "Once in a blue moon she will cry. She'll cry at stupid things – like when we leave to go somewhere.

"She's softened heaps since she's grown older. I can talk about things now in front of Nan that I would never talk about when I was young and I tease her heaps. She is always making us laugh because she repeats everything and you hear the same stories about four times a day."

Kerewai clearly has a soft spot for Rosie. "She's the baby of my eldest son's kids. She used to live in Auckland and now she has moved back home and married a Niuean boy, Lupe. He's a good fella. Rosie is a hardworking person. She has a nice nature. She always has. She has her own children and is a good mother."

While Kerewai appears to have the constitution of an ox, her grandchildren know she's not going to be around forever. But it's not something they can face thinking about.

"She's in good health," says Rosie. "She'll outlast all of us if she doesn't crash her car. But it won't be her fault!"

Ross McMillan & his grandchildren Jamie & Rae

Thunderclouds are tumbling into the skies over the Maniototo Plain, a landscape burnt golden by one of the hottest, driest summers in living memory. To an outsider, it looks as if the drought might be about to break.

But sheep farmer and poet Ross McMillan and his grandchildren Rae, 13, and Jamie, 11, barely glance upward, even as an eerie darkness descends on the bright March afternoon.

"It's closed in like this a few times and then it seems to just pass right over," Ross muses, unwilling or unable to let himself be too optimistic.

It's been a dreadful summer for Ross and many hill country farmers like him, struck by the worst drought the region has ever seen and, more recently, the menace of fire. Feed is still drastically short and in just one hour this morning, five sheep trucks have departed the region laden with sheep for sale or feeding outside the Maniototo.

"It's been desperate really," says Ross. "Creeks have stopped running in the plains that had never stopped running before. Stock prices have been so bad it's all been a bit of a bad year, but then we've had that before. I just look back to the old pioneers and what they put up with and think we are not so badly off after all."

But now, to top everything off, Ross's favourite horse, a placid white mare called Judal, almost died this morning. She was struck with a mystery illness that made her heart work so hard her frame shuddered with every beat. The vet guessed calcium deficiency and an injection appeared to relieve the symptoms, but Ross is still concerned.

When his grandchildren arrive after school (a short walk up the hill from the home they share with their father Peter), his mood lifts visibly and before long he shares the weight of his worry, telling them about the illness afflicting the 15-year-old mare who has been around longer than they have.

"I thought we were going to lose her," he tells the siblings, watching their faces. They blink, but say little. The pair take a few moments to check on Judal, gently stroking her neck, still stained with blood from the injection. Both of them learned to ride on the gentle horse, now standing with legs slightly splayed, head partially bowed. Yet barely a word is spoken about the mare.

"We're quiet people down here," muses Ross, and it's a fair comment. He and his grandchildren are quiet in their ways, their speech, and the care they take with each other. But there is no need for these three to put into words the deep affection between them.

Ross has been an idol for these children as long as they can remember, a hard-working farmer and poet known as "Blue Jeans," renowned in the region for his tales of the hill country, the pioneers, the horses, dogs and people he's known.

"We call him Lala," says Rae. "It's because when I was little I couldn't say Grandad. I used to say Lala and it just stuck."

With the break-up of their parents' marriage, the children have moved around a little within the district, but for most of their lives have been within walking distance of their grandfather. In fact, as soon as Rae could walk, the toddler used to climb the hill, push through Ross's fence and walk into his kitchen demanding ice-cream. Now almost 14, she has given up the ice-cream hunts, but she and Jamie still regularly head up to Lala's for a game of pool.

"I've taught them everything I know on how to be good and they can clean me up now," says Ross.

Jamie protests: "You can beat me sometimes!"

Even now at an age well past bedtime stories, the pair still giggle at the thought of Ross's mad, made-up stories about Harry the Hawk and Henrietta the Hawkess.

But then poets usually do tell a good yarn. It's a source of deep pride to Rae and Jamie that when Naseby School closed down recently (the roll was too small to justify the school's existence) Ross stood up in front of the whole community and read a poem he'd written called "Farewell to Naseby School".

Jamie, who's determined to be a farmer when he grows up, spends hours of his spare time on the 1620 ha family farm with his father and grandfather.

"I see myself in him a lot, chasing rabbits and that sort of thing," says Ross, but he hasn't set his heart on Jamie one day taking over the farm. He's all too aware that family farming units are becoming increasingly uneconomical. "He says he wants to be a farmer and that's what he's thinking at the moment. But they change when they get older. He could turn out to be a famous singer yet!"

Already Rae is thinking of a future outside the Maniototo, her desire to travel triggered by a cousin working as a nanny in the United States. Ross knows that the day will come when both his grandchildren will be too far away to pop up the hill for a game of pool and a story with Lala. But he won't be putting any pressure on them to stay. "We hope they are happy and healthy and that all their dreams come true. That's the main thing."

While he considers the future, heavy rain starts pelting the old homestead and the thunderstorm finally cuts loose. Now the kids are looking skyward, standing at the window to watch the lightning arcing through the black sky.

The drought is over.

Footnote: A few weeks later, a phone call to Naseby delivers good news and bad. The rain has kept falling and the Maniototo is bathed in green grass, "two to three inches high in places". But Ross's dear old mare Judal has died, five days after she first fell ill, of suspected kidney disease.

Roger Skinner & his grandson Cameron

Since giving up his day job as a mechanic more than 40 years ago, Roger Skinner's life has revolved around music. In his heyday he showed thousands of baby boomers a rocking good time at dance halls around the country. So, it's no coincidence that when his grandson Cameron comes to visit, it's not long before the music starts up.

"Cameron is three years old now, and now is the time to get him motivated into it," says Roger, pictured here teaching Cameron to pluck a few notes on a ukulele outside his parents' house truck.

Roger, now based in Helensville, says he's keen to pass on his passion for music, but there's no pressure to do anything but enjoy it. "He's a natural," smiles Roger. "He's got it in him I think."

Don Hopkins
& his grandson Andrew McQueen

reasure map: "Walk to the rock/Look to the wharf/Seven metres ye must walk/back towards the wharf/Probe and dig near the high tide mark"

Whoever thought you needed pricey computer games, designer building blocks and high-tech toys to entertain kids? Don Hopkins finds that investing a little time and imagination still works a treat to delight small children.

When Don's grandson Andrew had a pirate's party to celebrate his sixth birthday, Don sprang into action, building a treasure chest – complete with creaky lid and rope handles – and burying it deep in the sand at his local beach for the kids to discover.

A few days later, when his daughter Robyn arrived at Maraetai Beach with six little pirates in tow, the real life treasure hunt was organised. Pirate Don had raised the "Jelly Roger" flag on the bow of the ship-like adventure playground and, while the kids played, a message in a bottle mysteriously appeared on the beach.

"We had to go down the beach to find the bottle with the map to find the treasure," explains Andrew, adding that it was hard work for young pirates to find the exact spot on the map then pace out to where the treasure was buried.

"Then Dad and me hit the treasure with the spade!"

Inside the treasure box were some gold snack bars, drinks and "vittles vouchers" for the pirates to present at the local takeaway bar for their reward – hot dog and chips. The best part of the day? "Eating the food!" grins Andrew.

Like thousands of other New Zealand grandparents, Don lived through the poverty of the Great Depression and old habits die hard. He's still careful with money, is a squirrel-like hoarder and do-it-yourselfer who prefers to invest time rather than cash in his seven grandchildren.

"We really didn't have a penny to spend, so we had to make do with a lot of things," muses Don, a retired Baptist minister. "The money wasn't there to be buying toys."

But the lessons learned in those tough times mean Don knows how to entertain youngsters with whatever is at hand. "We have a good old time doing things," he says. "They love to come here and go bush walking. We look at the mosses and orange mushrooms and creepy crawlies. We do the best we can for them. I enjoy being a grandfather."

Ann Yates
& her granddaughter Tala

Ann Yates was less than impressed about becoming a grandmother. It was nothing personal, as she was instantly besotted with the baby girl her daughter Anna delivered on New Year's Day 1998 but, at the age of 46, she just wasn't ready to wear the "grandmother" label.

But, a few weeks after baby Tala's birth, Ann faced the awful possibility that Tala might not live long enough for her to say the dreaded word.

"The doctor picked it up at her six-week check and thought she had a hole in her heart, so she had a scan and literally within 48 hours she was in hospital."

As fluid gathered on Tala's lungs, doctors warned that the child's life was in danger and she would have to have open-heart surgery to correct the faulty valves – an extremely high-risk operation for such a young baby.

"The operation was a total success, but they say the first 24 hours can be really touch and go – and it was," says Ann. "We saw her after the surgery and she had this little beanie hat on with all the tubes on her. She was a good colour and we were just all so relieved, but the intensive care nurse said, 'You don't count your chickens yet because this is the time you can lose her.' And it almost was. It happened during the night and they had to reopen her and massage her heart. We were lucky not to lose her."

Thanks to the efforts of an expert surgical team at Greenlane Hospital and, Ann believes, gutsy determination on Tala's part, the baby pulled through and a few weeks after her first birthday shows no signs of any health problems, apart from the scar running down the centre of her chest.

"We call it her zip," laughs Ann. "But we had a good result and she's never looked back."

Ann recalls that even amid the crisis, she still couldn't quite spit out the G word. "When I had to phone up after the op – I was ringing up daily to see what was happening – I would say, 'This is the uh-uh' because I couldn't say it!"

She and Anna found a way to get around the problem – they've decided that Tala will call her Bomber – a name suggested by a friend.

"Anna looked at me and said, 'That is just so you; you are always on the move,' so I said, 'Okay we'll have Bomber' and it's sort of stuck."

Sylvia & Peter Siddell & their grandson Max

S ix-year-old Max Siddell sits at his grandparents' dining table gulping milk, chewing apple pieces and listening to them talk about him.

"He's lovely," says the boy's grandfather, Peter Siddell. "He's very interested in everything."

Grandmother Sylvia Siddell agrees. "He loves insects and natural history and parts of the body. He likes watching those documentary videos that you can hire. The last two were about Australian animals and Egypt, weren't they Max?"

The child nods sagely, commenting in a sing-song voice, "I store it all in my head."

The boy is the most junior member of what must be one of the most creative households in New Zealand. Peter and Sylvia Siddell are two of New Zealand's most celebrated artists. Peter is a realist artist who works in oils and pastels; Sylvia's style is expressive, using oils as well as acrylic, while their daughter Emily is a sought-after, emerging artist specialising in sculpture.

It's common for Max to return home from school to find two if not three artists hard at work. Max and his mother Emily Siddell inhabit the flat in the rear portion of Peter and Sylvia's rambling villa in Mt Eden, Auckland.

"People think he would be the centre of attention, but quite often we are all pre-occupied," says Sylvia.

Max agrees. "They are busy most of the time, but I can go and see them when they are working."

Rather than getting irritated about having a child in the house, Peter and Sylvia find they have become more patient with age.

"Your perspective on the world changes as you get older. You are getting toward the end of your life, which is very different to when you are in the middle of it," says Peter. "Your values get sorted out; what's important becomes much clearer. Of course the important things are human values, values of contact with people and primarily that's family – it always was of course, but when you are younger there are so many of the pressures coming down, with work and just making a living."

Sylvia nods. "Just never having a moment to yourself. I often resented having the children around because I really just wanted a little bit of time to myself." Both Sylvia and Peter's parents had died by the time Emily and her sister Avril arrived in the world, and the couple really felt their absence.

Now, she says, they're in an ideal position to not just enjoy Max's company, but provide a supportive "back stop" for Emily: the little things like picking him up from school, giving him a snack, entertaining him when she needs a night off and being there for advice.

"It spreads the responsibility," says Peter. "Because you've been around for a long time, you may not be any wiser, but you've seen a lot of things."

For Sylvia, one of the best things about Max is his great interest in natural history, something her own children had little interest in. "That's a great delight to me because that's one of my interests and my children didn't share my fascination, and I found it very frustrating," says Sylvia. "I would cart them down to the beach and show them the hermit crabs and they'd say, 'I want to go home and play with Barbie.'"

Max will quite happily spend an entire day exploring the Auckland Museum with his grandmother, or spotting cave wetas at the beach. "We saw a whole congregation of those striped cave wetas at Karekare and we raced back and got a torch and measured them. The biggest one was nearly 20 cm from the end of the antennae," says Sylvia.

Max's eyes widen at the memory: "Wooooooooow!" he says, reverentially.

On another occasion the family took a train up through the Waitakere Ranges and, with the lights and engine turned off, glided silently through a tunnel lined with glow worms. "Max said it was like flying in space and it was so real – the glow worms came right around you. He makes wonderful observations," says Sylvia.

The couple acknowledge there are some aspects of child-rearing they have no wish to experience again.

"The novelty of swings and slides is also long gone," she adds. "I found that got a bit tedious the first time around. I also wound up having terrible back problems and I realised it was lifting Max, because you are so used to picking a child up and putting him on your hip, and when you are 30 you can do that, but when you're closer to 60 you are not so bouncy."

While Max and Emily live under the same roof as Peter and Sylvia, their homes are essentially separate – which everyone appreciates.

"We are together a lot, but if Emily wants to be private or we want to be private we shut the door and it's taken for granted that we want to be private," says Sylvia.

Peter nods. "I think it would be very stressful if we were all living in the same house."

But neither of them resents interruptions if Max wants to pop in when they're working.

"We are used to this, we've grown up with it," smiles Peter, who has worked from home as an artist for 30 years, ever since his children were small. "When you don't have set hours to work, interruptions don't really matter because you can plan to work through in the evening."

Those interruptions can even be inspiring. A recent visit by Max to Sylvia's studio resulted in a wonderful painting called "Max Taming the Furies". The child had wandered in while she was listening to a stirring aria sung by a Welsh baritone telling the legend of Alexander the Great.

"It's very stirring music and Max was whizzing around flat-out on my office chair and I told him the music was about the legend of Alexander and burning down the palace and the furies were the dead Greek soldiers, but they have other meanings as well.

"Max said he could tame the furies and he showed me how he could do it, so he went and put on his armour, and then I added the colander because the proper helmets weren't the right shape, and gave him the vacuum cleaner pipe to hold, and did some drawings. He posed so well. You have to chase him around a bit while he's posing, but he's pretty good."

Sylvia has given the work an informal subtitle: "Max Tidies his Room". She also keeps a sketchbook started the day Max was born and adds to it whenever she remembers, while Peter's portrait of Emily and Max as a baby has pride of place in the living room.

So far Max hasn't shown a great deal of interest in drawing, but he has turned out to be a rather good art critic. "I did a painting of him quite a few years ago and he came in and looked at it and said, 'You've made me look like a doll. I don't look like a boy'," says Sylvia. "Another time I did some sketches of him and he said they were too old and they were. I had made the face too long. Often I ask his opinion on things. Those criticisms were very valid."

There's one more thing these two particularly like about young Maximillian Siddell: the names he calls them, Grandma and Grandad. "I like the name Grandad," says Peter. "When we had a young family it was common for our friends to be on first name terms with our children, but I thought, 'Everyone calls me Peter, but nobody else was ever going to call me Dad.' Same with Max. No one else is going to call me Grandad. Well maybe… who knows what the future holds?"

John Leask & his grandchildren Mason, Rhys & Tia

Seven-year-old Tia Leask thinks carefully before listing the reasons why her grandfather is one of her favourite people.

"Well, he's a nice man and he likes fishing and gardening," she says. "In the morning on my birthday he comes in and gives me a present. I've never seen him angry. He always wears blue and he wears a hat all the time. I think he has grey hair and he's bald – well I don't know if he's bald because he always wears a hat.

"He lives about three minutes' walk from us. He always gives us lollies and tells us to take a handful, and he gives us ginger beer and fizzy drink when we visit him."

John, a Stewart Island fisherman, has three grandchildren living on the island: Tia and her cousins Mason, eight, and Rhys, six. "They definitely keep you young," he smiles. "They're coming on and it's just great."

The children aren't yet old enough to realise it, but they're part of one of New Zealand's oldest European families. The little cove down the road from their grandfather's house offers a clue. It's called Leask Bay after John's great-grandfather, a blacksmith and shipwright who arrived on Stewart Island in 1850 direct from the Orkney Islands in Scotland. "He was given 20 acres of land so, like settlers do, they settled."

A century and a half later, Tia, Mason and Rhys are part of the sixth generation of Leasks to live on the island. John is so firmly planted in Stewart Island that he can't bear to uproot himself even for a few days. "I get quite upset even when I go to Invercargill for a few days. I don't think it's good really but you do get a bit tied to the place," he says.

However, there's no guarantee his grandchildren will feel the same way. "I wouldn't know whether they would stay here or not," he says. "Whatever suits them the best, but they will always have ties here.

"I've never really thought about whether there would always be Leasks on Stewart Island, but it would be nice. There are more young people here now than there were a few years ago, with a few mussel farms and a snapper farm which have employed a lot of people. Tourism is coming on quite a bit as well so that's helped pick things up."

Whether or not his grandchildren choose to spend their lives on Stewart Island, John knows they'll be staying put for at least another 10 years or so, and he plans to make the most of that time.

Millie Khan & her grandson Ryan

illie Khan was two minutes too late when she rushed into the Rotorua Hospital delivery suite to witness her daughter Marina give birth. The boy she affectionately recalls as "a little weed of a kid" had already made his entrance into the world without her.

But that was the only significant moment in Ryan's life that Millie has missed out on. Six years down the track they're as close as a grandmother and grandson can be.

She calls him the "love child" and likes the way he cracks her up. He calls her Nan and likes the way she smells.

They live five minutes' walk from each other in Matamata and unless Commonwealth Games medallist bowls champ Millie is competing out of town, they talk to each other every day.

"He's not Mummy's boy," explains Marina. "He's Nannie's boy. Ryan loves her to pieces. If he could live with her, he'd live with her before me.

"Right from when he was a little baby, Mum would be around my house, sometimes before six in the morning, and I used to be feeding him and she'd take over. I would have washing done ready to hang out and so she'd go and do that and when he finished feeding she would take him so I could go and have my shower. She's been there right through.

"Every morning he rings her up. He's six now and he must have been doing that since he was three. He asks her what she's been doing and whether she's coming down. If she comes down he says, 'Oh, you have to stay the night', so we have to go up to her house and lock up and turn off the lights so she can come back and stay the night. Or, if we go up there, he hides his pyjamas under his top so we end up staying."

Ryan's reasons for adoring his grandmother are simple.

"I like going to her house because I'm used to the smells," he explains. "I have this blanky and I still like it, but if I forget my one at home, Nan will give me one of

MATAMATA BOWLING CLUB

right and wanted to stay with her for a week."

There's nothing complicated about the relationship between the two.

"He's a very happy little boy. A good kid really," muses Millie, 60. "He's into everything. He plays a lot of sport. He plays rugby for the Midgets and he plays tennis and soccer."

Ryan Khan may also be New Zealand's youngest lawn bowls expert, having spent years following his grandmother around the Matamata Bowling Club as well as some of her out-of-town tournaments.

"Marina used to bring him down to the green when he was a baby. He sometimes gets on the green and plays with the jack and a couple of bowls and he tries to copy Nana's stance," smiles Millie. "He's a little hard case. He has his little carpet bowls and brings them here and plays on the lawn with them. He says, 'Nan, watch me drive.'

"He comes to the bowling club when we're playing a tournament and he's a good kid. He takes all his colouring pencils and what-have-you and talks to all the ladies. He never interferes when we are bowling. He's really good and all the women seem to like him."

The bright six-year-old has learned everything he knows about bowls from Nana.

"I like how you do the jack. Some of my friends throw it because they think it's a bouncy ball but I say to them, 'It's a bowling ball!'" he declares with an exasperated sigh. "My friend Tyler thinks my Nan plays ten pin bowling but I always say 'bowls!' back to him!"

But Millie has no particular desire for Ryan to follow in her footsteps and become a top international player. "Well really for his sake I hope he doesn't. I hope he gets

her scarves with perfume on it. That's why I always go to her house."

The other critical attraction is Millie's Milo-making skills. "She puts sugar in there," says Ryan. "Mum doesn't like sugar because my teeth might get rotten, but Nan likes putting sugar in because I like it."

Ryan is so attached to his grandmother that he's been known to pack a major sad when she heads out of town for bowling tournaments.

"When he was younger he went really strange on her after she'd been in Canada. He didn't want to stay with her. But he was in a snotty because she had left him so long!" laughs Marina. "After a couple of days he came into rugby because there's no money in bowls."

Another favourite activity for the pair is fishing. "The first year he was born we had his cot inside the van while we were whitebaiting down the Kaituna River at Maketu," says Millie.

"Ryan is a good fisherman. Not when he caught the eel though! A few weeks ago we were down the Kaituna River with our lines and it was just getting onto dusk and we had caught a couple of herrings. Next thing Ryan's line was pulling and he was saying, 'Mum! Mum! I think I've caught a kahawai.'

"Out comes this eel! Well… you should have seen him. He dropped the line. He'd never caught an eel before and he took off! It was so funny. We picked it up and took the eel back in the bucket with the hook and all. He was proud, yes. The next morning the eel was still on the hook so he stood on the chair holding onto it, so we have photos of him and his eel."

Marina says it's been wonderful to watch the close relationship develop between Ryan and her mum.

"He's probably the closest grandchild to Mum. The others have sort of missed out because Mum's been so busy. I think that's probably why she wants to retire because she has all these little ones coming along too and she's thinking, 'Well it's not fair.' She's missed out on the others."

Ryan is one of Millie's 19 grandchildren and she even has four great-grandchildren these days.

Thousands of New Zealanders remember sharing her grief over the loss of her 11-week-old grandson Brad to cot death the day she was due to play the singles final at the Auckland Commonwealth Games in 1990. Millie's family decided not to tell her about Brad's death until after she'd finished playing. She went on to win a silver medal.

"They kept that from me all day until after the final. I knew nothing about it and they did very well to hide it too," says Millie. "Was it the right thing to do? Well I don't know. I've had a lot of these questions asked in the letters people have sent from all over New Zealand. But who knows?"

As soon as she found out about Brad's death, Millie dedicated her bowls to her grandson and went on to win five major competitions, earning a gold star in her sport in just 13 months. She wonders whether knowing about Brad might have given her the extra determination to take away the gold medal that day.

"When I think back about it, if I had been told maybe I would have got an extra bit out of my bowls, but I don't know. I suppose it was the wisest thing they did. That was the first grandchild I lost so I felt it pretty hard. I still think about Brad, especially when it's around the Commonwealth Games times."

Now at the age of 60, Millie is planning to retire from international competition.

"I just feel like I've had enough," she muses. "There's a bit of pressure coming on now. They say, 'You have to come back with medals, blah blah blah,' and the fun has sort of gone out of it now so I thought, 'Blow this, I can do without all that.'"

The bonus of having all that extra time on her hands is that she'll be seeing a lot more of her grandchildren.

What does she think they'll remember of her when she's gone? Millie smiles. "Oh, being a good Nan I think…"

PONSONBY

Mike Gardner & his granddaughters Eloise, Alana, Sophie, Caitlin & Emma

Want to win the undying affection of your grandchildren? Cook them waffles - massive plates of the things loaded down with maple syrup or blueberries and cream.

Let them into your kitchen to spread eggs, flour and sugar all over the floor and then gather around the table letting everyone talk with their mouth full and help themselves to seconds, thirds and even fourths.

It has worked for West Auckland school principal Mike Gardner, who's earned major brownie points for his waffle-cooking marathons.

He makes buckets of waffle mix at a time to satisfy the appetites of his ravenous "sub-tribe" of girls.

"Well it's a Christmas morning tradition to cook waffles and basically I enjoy cooking – as you can tell!" he grins, affectionately patting his ample belly.

While Mike's wife, Nan, provides a quieter style of grandparenting – hours spent on artistic, gardening and outdoor pursuits (and cleaning up after waffle sessions), Mike prefers his grandparenting in shorter bursts – a reflection of the fact he works with children all day as principal of West Harbour Primary School.

"Nan is much better at grandparenting than I am. There are times when I just need my space if there are little people around because I work with little people all day," he says.

However, one of the things he appreciates most about being a grandparent is the opportunity to do things differently from the way he raised his own children, Georgia and Jessica.

"I was a typical '60s and '70s father. I was never there for the birth of my own children. Poor old Nan had to go through this whole birthing process on her own. But I've been there for the birth of all my grandchildren."

Canadian-born Mike also takes delight in the fact that his waffle-making sessions have given his grandchildren a taste of Canadian life – complete with the real Canadian maple syrup he serves with them.

It's almost 30 years since Mike emigrated to New Zealand with Nan (a New Zealander he met in Vancouver) but he'll never forget the first moment he laid eyes on New Zealand. "We were flying in over Raglan and all the Kiwis stood up in the plane and cheered. I thought, 'these people are mad!' It was really an amazing thing to see."

Mad they may be, but after the best part of three decades, Mike is an established member of the loony bin. "I get itchy feet when I'm away, I can't get back quick enough."

Like Mike and Nan, Georgia and Jessica have both married people from different backgrounds. Eloise and Alana's dad, Lucky, is Samoan, and Sophie, Caitlin and Emma's dad, Steven, is English.

"It's kind of nice because two of our granddaughters are half-Samoan and the other three are English primroses," says Mike. "It's a really nice mix of cultures."

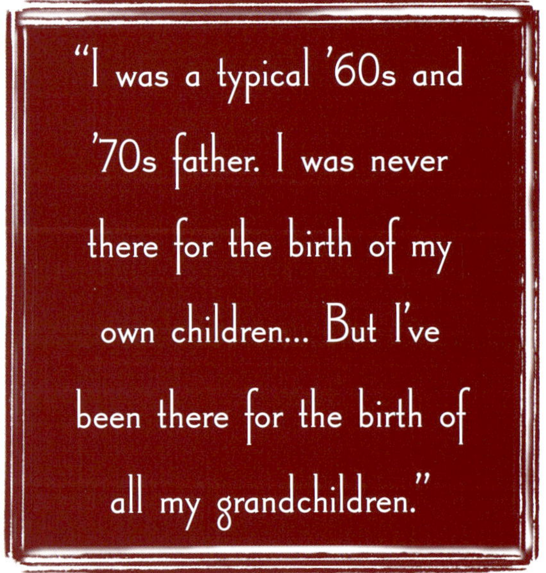

Mike Gardner's Soon-to-be-famous Waffle Recipe

INGREDIENTS
6 cups flour
4 tsp baking powder
1 tsp salt
4 tbsp sugar
3 cups milk
6 large eggs (separate whites from yolks)
1 cup butter

COOK'S TIP
The secret to waffles is separating the eggs because you beat the whites
into the old pavlova stuff and fold that into the mixture. That's what gives
it the bubbles.

METHOD
Mix the dry ingredients in a large bowl. Separate the eggs. Beat the egg
whites until they're white and fluffy. Melt the butter. Mix the egg yolks, melted
butter and milk together. Add that to the dry ingredients and mix. Carefully fold
beaten egg whites into the mixture. Heat up the waffle iron and put two
spoonfuls of mix in each side. Cook for four to five minutes. Remove and serve
with real maple syrup – the Canadian stuff. Alternatively, serve with whipped
cream and blueberries or boysenberries.

COOK'S TIP NUMBER TWO
If you are a true Canadian, you have bacon and sausages and
scrambled eggs on the side.

Lesley Ford
& her grandson Callum Turner

Time is too precious for Lesley Ford to waste worrying about dying. But every now and then she gets a sharp reminder about the illness which is robbing her of the chance to grow old with her grandchildren.

"The only time I get really angry is when I see a little, grey-haired, old lady with a 12 or 14-year-old grandchild walking down the street and I feel: 'I don't think I'm ever going to have that' and I get a bit cross I'm never going to be a proper grey-haired nana. Then I have to try very hard to be grateful but it's hard to be grateful.

"When I first became sick and the doctor told us, I burst out crying and [when he asked me why], I said, 'All I wanted to do was be a granny,'" she recalls. "He said, 'Right! We'll have to make you a granny' and my daughter wasn't even married! I said, 'Right, if you can get me to be a granny I'll shout you the best bottle of champagne I can find and a lovely morning tea!'"

For the next few years and especially after Nicola married, the whole thing became a great joke between doctor and patient. "Every time I visited him he would say, 'Is she pregnant yet?' I would say, 'No! I've been threatening to put holes in my son-in-law's condoms!' and he used to laugh."

Finally, in December 1997, Lesley delivered a bottle of Moet and a huge cheeseboard to the doctor to celebrate the fact that Nicola was expecting her first child in March.

"Callum is very special," she says. "I was in hospital when he was born. One of the nurses came along to me in hospital and said, 'Good morning Gran.' Nikki had been up there for 12 hours and I didn't know. They took me around in the wheelchair to see her, so I saw him about 15 minutes after he was born to give him a cuddle.

"I never cried. I can't believe I never cried. But it's such a wonderful experience. Who wants to spend their time crying? It's so great."

Lesley says Callum, who was five months old when this picture was taken, is a delight. "He's a little fellow with a beautifully proportioned body. He's going to be tall like his dad, Campbell, who's six foot two or three. He's 11 months now and he has the most beautiful set of eight teeth and a happy smile. He loves music and he's standing up and just about to walk.

"He's a wonderful eater and has a neat sense of humour. I think he might have a little temper – I'm not sure. I don't think there's anything extra special about him. He's just a cute wee fellow."

Lesley believes one positive aspect of her illness has been that she's had to give up work, so she's been able to be more like her own mother with more time to spend with her children and grandchild rather than always being busy and tied up with work. Despite the debilitating tiredness caused by the illness and the treatment – Lesley spends one week in every three in hospital – she's forever using what little energy she has on gran-like activities: baking cookies, knitting clothes and buying presents.

"My mother was a wonderful nana. All our children loved her that much. I used to think if I could be half or quarter as good as my mum, I would be pretty special because she was a special lady. The sons-in-law thought the world of her.

"I look around me and the grandparents today are often working. If I wasn't sick I wouldn't be doing these things. So really everybody has benefited."

The old cliche of taking time to smell the roses is something Lesley and her husband, Rowan, have taken to heart since she's been sick. "My husband spends more time with Callum than he did with his own kids.

"When I look back [as a parent] I never spent the time. I was always too busy. Probably being sick has taught me that life is precious and unfortunately no matter how often you are told you don't hear. You can listen but you don't hear. I find that a lot when I talk to people about it. They listen but you can see in their eyes that they've already moved on to the next thing.

"It's something I've learned with Callum – things like rushing around and tidying up the house or putting the dinner on are not important when he comes around. I like to spend time with him. I can't lift him as well now. My hips are gone. But I pop him in the pushchair and take him out to the garden. I love dancing with him and singing, playing music. I taught him all the rude noises with his tongue!"

Lesley sees Callum every day of the week and he and his mum always visit her in hospital. "He thinks the drip trolley is a wonderful thing. He jumps on top of me and gives me millions of bruises," she grimaces.

Despite all the good things, she is careful to avoid looking too far into the future – about the possibility of a sister for Callum or seeing her son Julian marry and have children.

"There is no cure for this disease. Some people do really well and some don't. I'm one of the few that has managed to fight it off since 1992. Apparently that's very unusual. I've done very well. But I'm stubborn.

"I have three-monthly goals. I did that right from the beginning and I thought I would find that really hard. But I don't. If there's nothing happening for six months I hop on a plane and go and see my sister in Central Otago. I do something all the time that's special – and I think that helps because you always have something to look forward to."

But Lesley can't help being conscious of how much she has to cram into the time she has left.

"It's nearly March. It feels like yesterday we had our first Christmas with Callum. All of a sudden I feel like time seems stolen from me and I don't like that feeling and I try not to think about it. It is precious with Callum as it is with both my children and my son-in-law. I might never see if Nikki has any more children. I might never see my son marry or have children and that's where I find stealing of time quite sad because nobody can control that."

One thing Lesley knows for sure is that Callum will never forget her.

"My daughter is always going to bring up things and say, 'I can remember when Gran and I did things.' Nicola will never let my memory go."

> "When I look back I never spent the time. I was always too busy. Probably being sick has taught me that life is precious and unfortunately no matter how often you are told you don't hear. You can listen but you don't hear."

Mark Allen & his grandfather Harry

When the All Blacks have a bad day, the whole nation seems to take it personally. But it would be a brave fan indeed who would front up, face to bulging pectorals, to an individual player like former All Black Mark "Bull" Allen to give him a few pointers on where he went wrong in the game.

Strangely enough, Mark's critics never had a problem sharing their views with his grandfather, Harry Allen.

The 82-year-old, who still works in the family auto-electrical business, is a great fan of rugby and he became used to hearing all about it when Mark played at less than his awesome best for Taranaki or New Zealand.

"I always used to tell everybody when Mark wasn't playing so well that he has trouble with his breathing – he's not an asthmatic, but he has an asthma problem. That's probably why he has an off day. I've always made excuses for him in that way."

Sitting in his grandfather's sunny lounge in New Plymouth, Mark shrugs his shoulders. It's a familiar story. "I do use inhalers and things, yes, but it's funny how no one would ever come up to me and say to my face, 'You played badly', but they'd say it to Poppa."

But Harry was never fazed by the criticism. "You have to take these things as they happen. It's just part of life."

Harry is, of course, one of Mark's biggest fans, although he's at pains to point out that he and his wife, Irene, have never gone in for favouritism among their 11 grandchildren.

Looking back, the thing Harry remembers most clearly about Mark as a child is, ironically, his hair. Ironic because for most of his adult life Mark has had a shaved head.

"He had absolutely pure blonde curly hair. He could have been a girl he was so… so…."

Mark jumps in, "Good looking is the word you're looking for!"

Harry: "Yes, I'd say that. Too good looking for a boy."

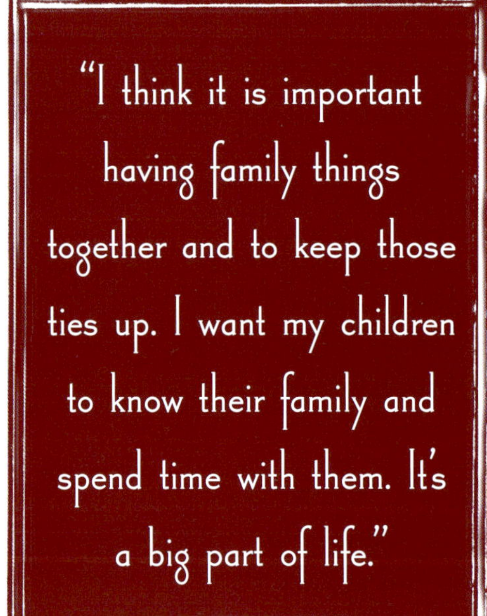

And was this good-looking boy well behaved? "When he was asleep," says Harry dryly. "He was always so active. He was always on the go. His first job that I can remember was on the milk run in Stratford. That's how I reckon he developed his physical ability. He used to run with the trolley to keep up with the truck. He was also into wrestling when he was at high school, and it was that and the weightlifting which helped him develop his strength."

But Harry also has another theory.

"I'm not bragging, but I could show you a newspaper clipping about my great-grandfather. He was supposed to be the strongest man in Taranaki in his youth."

Sure enough, he hunts out a well-worn file filled with newspaper clippings and old photographs. He pulls out the copy of an article, probably from New Zealand's first newspaper, the now defunct *Taranaki Herald*.

"He was noted for the tremendous movement he took with the scythe and for his stamina," the clipping reads.

"I reckon that's where Mark has got his strength from," says Harry. "Most of our family are – well they're not delicate, put it that way. I'm really the last one left now, but most of us have lived a long life and my half-sister lived until she was in her 90s. I put it down to the fact the family are real pioneers."

However, one thing Mark hasn't inherited from his great-great-grandfather is the sternness emanating from William Allen's photograph. Mark's easy-going, cheerful nature is the thing his grandfather likes most about him.

"Everybody likes him," says Harry. "He has a great way with children. He has a very boyish sort of way with him too. He's not serious and most of our family are fairly serious. He's always been… shall we say, a free spirit. He's not frightened to express that."

Mark's earliest memories of his grandparents go back to the Taranaki beach settlement of Oakura, where Harry and Irene had a bach for many years before eventually retiring to the area.

"We went there quite a lot as kids so I remember we used to have big family parties," says Mark. "They used to love music; they always had the music playing – lots of jazz and Louis Armstrong, and there used to be a lot of singing.

"I think it was a wonderful environment and certainly something I would like to have with my children as well. I think life can be so serious and it's great to have a lot of those nice, relaxed fun times. Life revolves around working and trying to make money, so just things like that are a great way to forget your responsibilities and just enjoy things."

The only time Harry can recall being seriously upset with Mark was when he shaved off his hair that first time.

"Well for a start I didn't like it," he says frankly. "In his early days the only people that had their hair done like that were the skinheads. I was disgusted. I was thinking, 'What's he doing?' But now everybody has shaved heads."

Mark certainly remembers raising a few eyebrows when he first let loose his trademark bald head on the world.

"Maybe it was trying to be a bit different, I don't know. I remember when I was young I had quite a few hassles as a teenager because I had short hair. But bald-headed bull's heads are a very common part of everything now." However, he didn't hear a word of criticism from his grandfather.

Harry says he would never have shared his feelings with Mark. "I would never be critical. That's his life."

That non-critical approach is something Harry has worked hard at. He acknowledges his own grandmother was a "dour" woman and he didn't want to have the same sort of reputation in the lives of his grandchildren.

Mark and his cousins have reaped the benefits of that attitude, and Mark appreciates it even more now that he has children of his own. "It's hard when you have young children – you can't take them just anywhere because some people are very particular about their possessions, which is fair enough. But it's nice and relaxed for the kids to come here."

Mark, whose All Black career ended in the 1998 season when he suffered a major back injury, is busier than ever with a range of projects and promotional commitments. However, he's determined to make more time to spend with his grandparents.

"I have found it hard over the years because I haven't had a lot to do with Nana and Poppa because I've been away a lot and have been so busy. But I think it is important having family things together and to keep those ties up. I want my children to know their family and spend time with them. It's a big part of life."

Mark is even looking forward to being a grandfather himself one day. "I'd love to. I was just saying last night that I hope when our kids have kids that we have a big involvement with them."

Stewart & Jenny Macqueen & their granddaughters Estelle & Keziah Peters

Jenny Macqueen's teenage children used to cringe with embarrassment when she'd turn up to their school on a motorbike, clad in tight-fitting jeans and woolly "ug" boots.

"I wasn't like everyone else's mum," she grins. "Mums were supposed to wear pinnies and nice clothes to school meetings."

Now, at 52, Jenny is a grandmother and the ug boots have long since disappeared from her wardrobe.

But don't for a moment think she's stopped rebelling against stereotype. How many grandmothers do you know who spend their weekends clad in black leather and roaring around on a powerful 1340 cc Harley Davidson motorcycle?

Jenny, a sterilising technician, and her husband, Stewart, 50, a hotel maintenance manager, are members of the Ulysses motorcycle club. Its motto is "Grow Old Disgracefully" – something this couple cheerfully live by every day of their lives. And their 14 grandchildren? Well, they're welcome to come along for the ride.

Between them, the Macqueens have five motorbikes: three Harley Davidsons, a Suzuki Low Rider and a '58 Velocette undergoing restoration. Their ultimate aim is to have as many bikes as they have grandchildren.

But in a classic case of history repeating itself, some of their eldest grandchildren are just reaching the age where the very things that delighted them in childhood – such as grandparents who cruise around on Harley Davidsons are starting to lose their appeal.

Sitting in the lounge at Stewart and Jenny's Whangaparaoa home, two of those grandchildren, Estelle, 13, and Keziah, 11, are sympathising with a story about their Aunty Marnie. Marnie used to pretend not to recognise her mother when Jenny sped past the school bus on the motorbike wearing those trademark ug boots.

Would Estelle find it embarrassing? "It's even more embarrassing," she groans with a glint in her eye. "Why?

Because they're my *grandparents*!"

She doesn't mean it in all seriousness – yet. As Jenny reminds her granddaughter, it was only a few weeks ago that she was on the back of Jenny's bike whooping and hollering: "Nana, Nana, go faster! Don't let Poppa overtake us!"

"When they become teenagers, their whole attitude starts to change," says Jenny, a tad wistfully. "Then it's not really that cool to go out on bikes with Nana and Poppa."

However, Jenny is confident that the embarrassment will be shortlived. After all, Estelle has been out with her grandparents on their bikes since she was six years old and her legs were at last long enough to reach the pedals. The motorbike bug is in her genes.

"Estelle used to go to sleep on my FJ 1200," says Stewart. "I used to have to ride with one hand holding her on the back going up the Albany hill. I'd get a whack in the back of the head and have to hold on to her. She was about six or seven at the time."

It's something of an irony that Estelle and Keziah's mother, Blanche, has never been a big fan of motorbikes – but she's swallowed her fears to allow her parents to share their passion for bikes with their grandchildren. "I don't actually like motorbikes," she confesses. "I feel really naked. It's not my thing and I do worry about the kids but it's not Mum and Dad – it's the other drivers."

Blanche just keeps reminding herself that accidents can happen anywhere – even to kids walking along the footpath. "Just because I don't personally like going out on the bikes a lot shouldn't mean they miss out."

Jenny and Stewart are at pains to point out that they never speed – at least not with the grandchildren on board! "We never really go very fast," says Jenny. "If the kids are on the bikes with us, we are very sensible. It would be tragic if anything happened. You just cruise and enjoy the scenery."

The Macqueens tend to take the grandchildren with them on special rallies – such as the popular Toy Run where around 1500 bikies ride two abreast from Cambridge to Hamilton collecting toys for children with cancer.

However the bikes are only one facet of the relationship between Jenny and Stewart and their grandchildren. With Estelle and Keziah living close by, they see the girls at least twice a week, and the pair often spend Friday nights at their grandparents' house – as do all the other grandchildren.

"They like coming over here and staying," says Stewart. "There are five kids in the family and they're at a stage now of wanting to have a bit of space – so we'll take them up to the Plaza or whatever."

The first thing the girls tend to do when they walk into their grandparents' house is raid the pantry.

"Last week Estelle turned up and said: 'Nana everything in your fridge is healthy! It's all crispbread and hummus!'" Jenny laughs. She inevitably ends up stocking up on soft drink, milo and chocolate biscuits for when the grandchildren visit.

Jenny and Stewart are all too aware that as Estelle and Keziah grow up, those Friday nights will probably diminish as other attractions take over but they're not worried about it. "We feel lucky in that as the older grandchildren grow up and become more independent there are still lots more waiting in the wings to keep Nana and Poppa company on and off the bikes," smiles Jenny.

She and Stewart readily acknowledge they're far softer

on their grandchildren than their children.

"I would say our grandkids know that we are more pliable than parents," says Stewart, who has been a born-again Christian for 30 years. "It's the old adage that you can hand them back, but I think they do become more like friends than your own kids."

Jenny agrees. She was present at the birth of Keziah and four of her other grandchildren. "There is a certain bond when you are actually there and see that grandchild born. You can't help having a special feeling for the child."

What's more, she and Stewart worry a lot about their grandchildren growing up in a country they fear is far more hazardous than the New Zealand they grew up in, with greater peer pressure on young people, easy access to drugs and rising crime rates.

"I would be far more protective of my grandchildren than I was of my own children," says Jenny, also a born-again Christian and former industrial chaplain. "I think as you get older you are more aware of the dangers and pitfalls in life. I was young when I had my children and worked the whole time while raising a family and it was a matter of just absolute survival and keeping the family together. I don't think I stopped and thought about the dangers there for the kids. I just didn't have the time! But when you have grandchildren you have got all the time in the world to think and you are so much more aware of the dangers out there.

"You would like to take them all off to an island where nobody can get to them and keep them all cocooned until they get to about 21."

However, the couple have confidence in the parenting skills of their own children and feel sure the grandchildren won't go "off the rails". They're more concerned about the dangers of placing high expectations on the children. Stewart feels particularly strongly about this. Having always been regarded as a rebel, he's spent his life fighting stereotypes: he's a long-haired, leather-wearing biker who's also a dedicated family man and committed Christian. "Rebelliousness is actually a state of individualism," he says. "People try to put you into the mould but you should be yourself, totally yourself." He wants to ensure his grandchildren have the same freedom.

"We don't look at the outside of the person as we're more interested in the inside. I don't mind what these kids want to do as long as they are happy. If they want to be successful in something or have a goal, I'll support them as much as I can but if they don't want to set a goal and just go through life to be happy, that's fine too. Why should we put expectations on our children or grandchildren to their own detriment? They can do what they want to do."

Jenny feels a little differently. "I probably have higher expectations," she says. "I would like them to be… well what I think of as being successful in life, which may not be what they think. To put it in a nutshell, to me every grandchild is a gift from God and they are very precious, they are all individuals, they've all got characters of their own and you can see each one of them developing differently."

And how would this couple like to be remembered? "I'd like them to remember having a good time with us," says Stewart.

Jenny nods. "I just want them to remember Nana as very special and that she had a good input in their lives." She looks across at Estelle and Keziah. "You'd better think that!"

NO. 2 WELLINGTON
SQUADRON
BATTERY
NO STEP
NEW ZEALAND

Pat Dunn
& his grandson Robert Way

At 10 years old, Robert Way's mind is filled with images of hostile aliens, space, time travel and futuristic weaponry – all part of the fantastic world of computer games he inhabits for much of his spare time.

Perhaps that is why he doesn't get quite as enthusiastic as his grandfather Pat Dunn at the thought of a flying machine that was built back in the 1930s.

But that doesn't stop Pat, 73, from sharing his passion for Catalina flying boats. He believes that given time, Robert will appreciate the marvels of the machine.

Pat is part of a syndicate of enthusiasts which brought a Catalina to New Zealand in 1994. The craft is thought to be the only one of its kind still flying in the South Pacific and Robert is one of the few New Zealanders who has ever flown in one. While excited at the time of his first flight in the Catalina, Robert's daydreams about technology seem firmly planted in the future rather than the past.

But Pat isn't disheartened.

"When he gets a bit older he'll look back into the history a little bit. When it's talked about he'll be able to say he flew in one because it's very rare."

There is, Pat points out, no shortage of excitement in the Catalina story. "It was one of the well-known planes of the war for rescues. When people were shot down in the sea, the Catalinas were sent in to bring them out. The Americans had a squadron called the Black Cats which could go in at night."

As he spins his yarns, Pat's eyes light up with a boyish excitement he's had about flying boats since a warm day early in 1937 when he joined crowds of people to view a trailblazing American Clipper seaplane at the Auckland waterfront – the first to make the journey all the way from America.

Back in those days helicopters, Concorde jets and even modern airports were the stuff of science fiction, so the boy could only marvel at the sheer size of the machine and how far it had travelled. He's been dotty about flying boats ever since.

Whether Pat's grandson Robert will still be talking about the Catalina in 60 years' time remains to be seen.

Sol Filler
& his grandson
Ron Haver

When Ron Haver celebrates his 17th birthday in 2002, he'll be surrounded by family and friends, weighed down with gifts, and have every reason to look forward to his next six years on the planet. Intelligent and articulate, he'll probably go on to some form of tertiary education, will grow independent, perhaps leave the family home, travel overseas, fall in love... the opportunities are endless.

For Ron's grandfather, Sol Filler, those same critical years, from the age of 17 to 23, offered just two possibilities: to live or to die.

Sol grasped life with every ounce of strength he could muster and luck was on his side. He is one of the minority of Polish Jews who survived to bear witness to the worst horrors of the Holocaust as Hitler's Nazi regime set about destroying the Jewish race.

In those desolate days after the war, Sol faced life without a family, a country or a future; his only possession the memories of the death camps, the massacres, the savagery he'd seen. It was difficult for him to imagine ever being happy again, let alone being part of a large, noisy family, full of hope for the future.

Yet here he is, half a century and half a world away from those days, sitting on a comfortable couch next to his grinning grandson, telling jokes, arguing good-naturedly with his wife, and optimistic that his descendants have a bright future in New Zealand.

Perhaps that is why, far from being a bitter man, Sol is a delight to be around, his sense of humour looming far larger in his family's eyes than his sadness about the past.

Ron sums it up well. "One of my earliest memories is when he showed me a mouse trick where he would make a mouse out of a handkerchief and pretend it was real and flick it up his arm. I thought for a while it was real," he smiles. "He's told me a lot of funny stories and a lot of Jewish jokes. There was one he told me the other day. It was about a rabbi, a priest and an Anglican minister and they were all sitting playing cards…"

The boy trails off and turns to his grandfather, "What happened again?"

Sol settles back in the couch, clears his throat, lifts his chin and with the unhurried pace of a seasoned joke teller, recites the tale flawlessly in his still heavy Polish-Jewish accent. The pair chuckle away together before returning to the topic at hand: Ron's impressions of his grandfather.

Ron pauses for a moment, pondering what to say next.

"Do you respect me? Do you love me?" Sol prompts, eyebrow raised.

Ron: "All those things. I respect him, I love him."

Sol nods solemnly: "I'm generous," he adds, turning to his grandson. "Am I generous?"

Ron: "Yes, he's very generous. When I was little he always used to bring presents for me and all of us. One time he came home with three ukuleles because I wanted to play the guitar and I used to practise on my tennis racket."

They look good together, these two, the bonds between them almost palpable. These bonds also extend through the entire family to Sol's wife, Ruth, their daughters, Deborah and Esther, Esther's husband, Arnon, and their three grandchildren including Ron and his sisters Samara, 13, and Daniella, 10.

A shared culture, religion and tragic family history have ensured that members of this family don't take each other for granted.

Born and raised in the peaceful village of Brzozow in

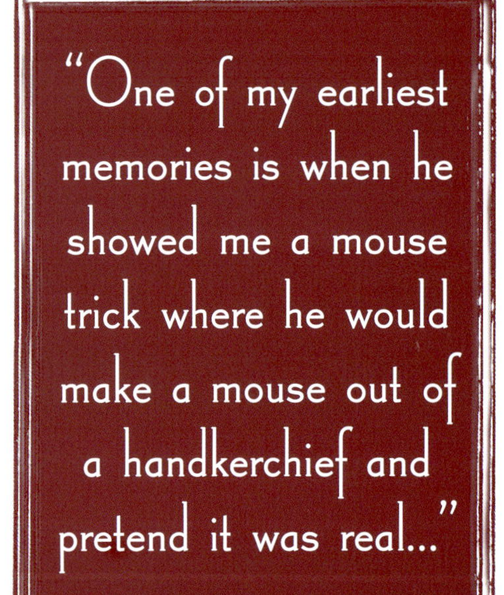

Southern Poland, Sol Filler's experiences of the Nazi regime are typical – which makes them all the more chilling. Most of his extended family were slaughtered in a single day in a massacre in the forest outside Brzozow in 1941. Sol and his younger brother Ben survived because they were already imprisoned in Plaszow, the concentration camp run by the sadist Amon Goeth and featured in the film *Schindler's List*.

Later they were transported to an even more frightening destination, Auschwitz, the death camp where hundreds of thousands of Jews were either gassed, executed, starved or worked to death. In Sol's six-year nightmare, more than half of which he spent imprisoned, he was treated as a slave, humiliated, beaten, kicked, shot at and starved. At Brzozow, he dug graves for pathetic Russian prisoners of war standing waiting to be executed. Later he took refuge for a few desperate months in the sewers surviving on scraps he risked his life to beg for. In Plaszow, he saw Amon Goeth taking pot-shots at children with a sniper's rifle. At Auschwitz, he saw the smoke rising from the crematoriums and saw Jews shot dead for crimes as trivial as a smile.

But his worst ordeal came just a few months before liberation, when the Nazis, aware that the end was near, evacuated Auschwitz. Sol and Ben were among thousands of sick and starving inmates who were marched hundreds of miles through the bitter Polish winter to Czechoslovakia and another camp, Terezin.

"Although I went through hell in Auschwitz, the worst time was when they took us away," says Sol. "Thousands of us left Auschwitz but very few arrived at the destination. They took us from January to May, four months without food, without drinks, without sleep, without everything. If you couldn't walk, they shot you. They couldn't leave you half-dead – if you sat down or lay down they killed you. So you walked, you walked, you walked over bodies practically the whole time."

Sol has no idea how he survived the ordeal – especially considering he escaped and was caught at one point. "I thought I was going to be executed. I was very lucky because the man who caught me – I still don't know to this day if he made a mistake or the guard made a mistake – but they took out another guy they thought was me and they shot him. They killed him."

Sol's philosophy throughout those years was a simple one. "You thought you were going to die, there's no doubt about it, but you still couldn't do much about it either. You were just completely helpless. We just… how can I say it? We just left it up to fate. Whatever will happen will happen."

Because of his philosophy, Sol was shocked after the war to hear that many Jews, having survived the horrors of the death camps, had breakdowns and committed suicide. But there were many unexpected aftermaths – such as the unspoken rule for many years that survivors didn't talk about their experiences. It was a phenomenon Sol noticed immediately after liberation when he spent four years in a displaced persons' camp in Germany.

"We never talked about the past, none of us. We talked about the future, what's going to happen, where are we going to be, where are we going to finish up, but we never talked about the past. I don't know why not. At the time I thought it was a little bit sad."

Not talking about the past became a habit for Sol, who

migrated to Australia after the war, eventually meeting his wife, Ruth, and moving to New Zealand. It was only when his eldest daughter, Deborah, a teacher, asked him to tell his story to her class that he decided to break his silence. "It wasn't easy but it was easier than I thought it was going to be. Since then people have asked me to talk about it and I talked about it."

While Sol is comfortable, even relaxed, in talking about the past, the horrors will always be with him. "I used to have a lot of nightmares but then I went back to Poland in 1975 for the first time, back to Auschwitz and to my own town and after that the nightmares stopped. They still come back occasionally but not as often as at the beginning."

What is more, the Holocaust is the very reason he and his descendants live at the opposite end of the earth to where it took place. "I could have gone to America or Israel but I chose the furthest place away," he says. "I thought the further away it is the better it is. If you read European history it's always wars, wars, always wars and slaughtering people. It's happening now in Kosovo."

Ron has always been interested in hearing about his grandfather's experiences. "He has told me a lot of stories and in class I was at a much higher level than other kids when we studied the Holocaust. I've read lots of books about it and he's really inspired me to learn a lot. I consider myself very lucky to know what went on there, to have him as my grandfather because I can probably tell my grandchildren that I had a grandfather who survived and he helped his brother survive as well."

While it's important to Sol that Ron knows about his experiences, he is equally determined not to leave behind a legacy of sadness. Hence his focus on the positive things in life: humour, acceptance of other people and the importance of family.

Ron: "One of the main lessons Grandad has taught us is stay close to your family. He's taught me things from the prayer book, he's taught me his old tricks that I will probably teach to my grandchildren and he's taught me a lot of general knowledge and morals as well. One of the most important things in Jewish faith is respect thy neighbour, which means you should respect everybody in the world no matter what. For instance I don't go around criticising other religions."

Friday night, the Jewish Sabbath, is family night for the Fillers and Ron's upbringing has ensured he has no complaints about staying home on a night many non-Jewish teenagers would rather be out with their friends.

"Of course sometimes I want to go out on Friday nights and sometimes I'm allowed to but only if it's a special occasion."

Ron's grandmother, Ruth Filler, adds: "We are not religious but we are very traditional. Friday night is a traditional thing where the family is together and also Passover and Jewish New Year. We spend those times together and my daughters and now the children too feel that family is the most important thing there is. If you don't hold closely to your family then you don't have much else."

While Sol loves all his grandchildren, he admits Ron is particularly special because he is the only grandson, and Sol never had any sons of his own. It's a great delight for him to be able to sit at Ron's side in the Orthodox synagogue, where men and women are separated during services.

He sees his role in Ron's life as a backstop to his father, Arnon. "I would say that the grandfather, especially the Jewish grandfather, is the double insurance. The grandfather usually is retired and he just has time to oversee things whereas the father might not have so much time because he's working. I'm fond of the grandchildren very much. We try to give them as much love as we can. They come here for a while, they go, it's quiet again. That's why I think grandparents are more fond of grandchildren than their own kids because they come, they go and finish!"

Now, at 76, Sol is facing another life and death battle – this time with cancer. Not surprisingly, his come-what-may philosophy hasn't changed.

"People say to me now, because I'm not a well man, 'Look, you overcame all those things before, you'll overcome this too' but it's a different thing altogether. Those days I was fighting a tyrant and I was young and fit. Now I'm fighting nature, which is a different thing altogether. I'm 76 now and I've had a good life so I can't do much about it."

The illness has brought Sol and Ron even closer. "I try to spend more time with him," says Ron, adding that he and Sol were disappointed that a planned family trip back to Poland had to be cancelled because of Sol's illness.

"I was looking forward to it," says Ron. "But the Jews are strong believers in fate and it wasn't meant to be."

For now, his grandfather is still around, full of energy, telling his jokes and keeping everyone amused.

"I haven't really thought about what it will be like when he's gone," says Ron. "No matter what, I will always remember who he was. I've always got photos and videos of him and I will remember his tricks so he will still live in me."

"One of the main lessons Grandad has taught us is stay close to your family. He's taught me things from the prayer book, he's taught me his old tricks that I will probably teach to my grandchildren…"

Jane Dent & her grandmother Vi Donaldson

It's Friday night in Auckland and just half an hour to go before live coverage of the Chiefs vs Blues Super 12 match starts. Jane Dent and her grandmother Vi Donaldson are settling into comfortable chairs in Jane's Herne Bay lounge and, with cups of tea and a snack on the table, are ready to watch the game.

Jane contemplates her grandmother across the coffee table and says what she's been itching to say about one of the most cherished people in her life.

"For me she's a role model for older people. I want to be like Vi when I get old," she says of the silver-haired, impeccably dressed 89-year-old. "She's so positive, she is so outgoing and independent and nothing is a problem and she always looks on the bright side of situations and she's just fantastic."

Vi is smiling back at her granddaughter but she's only picking up every few words because, typically as it turns out, she's left her hearing aid at home.

Jane continues, "I think part of it is because she's had a really tough life. Her father died when she was very young and her husband had a major drink problem. They had a pretty difficult history together and Vi moved out on a few occasions and so it was pretty hard."

She surprises herself when her emotions get the better of her and she is unable to speak for a few moments. Moving across the room she puts her arms around her grandmother, who pats her hand reassuringly and, bewildered, says, "Oh Jane, I can only hear part of what you're saying!"

Jane retorts, "Just as well! I'm just saying you are very special and I think you are very strong and very kind."

Vi smiles, "Oh and so are you, Jane."

The lessons Jane learned "by osmosis" from Vi's struggles will stay with her for life. "It made me think that whatever relationship I ended up in had to be a really, really good one. That's one of the really important lessons she taught me."

But Vi is quick to point out that it wasn't all a struggle.

There were a lot of good times and laughter as well – something Jane remembers well.

As a child growing up in Raglan, she had one set of grandparents (her father's parents) living close by and a second set living in Auckland. "When I was a child I thought everyone had a Grandma and Grandpa and a Nana and George," she says. "We never called George Grandpa and it sort of followed on in the family because I always call Vi's daughter, my mother, Jean."

Her earliest memories of Vi and George are of their visits to Raglan and Christmas and birthday letters and cards with "lovely, curly writing" and money or stickers tucked inside. She also has fond memories of visiting the pair when they lived in a house in the bush at Oratia in West Auckland. "I can still remember the smell in the laundry in that house. The soapy smell of your childhood. Occasionally in life you smell something and think, 'Oh, I remember that,' and it takes you right back to that moment of being in the laundry downstairs."

Despite his flaws, George had his good points. "George was a great man, he was a wonderful man. He just had this terrible problem," says Jane. "He was very bright and very interested in the world. He was a comedian. We had a lot of laughs with him and a lot of good times. Vi divorced him when he had a problem and then later on remarried him, but he still had the drink problem didn't he?" Vi nods. "He tried to [give up] but he couldn't really in the end. But still we had a lot of fun. He was a great dancer. Oh, yes."

She reminisces back to a crowded Lewis Eady dance hall when she and George rushed onto the dance floor as soon as the band started up. "People just sat there and watched us. I said to George, 'If you act the goat I'll go crook!', so he danced all right and they all stood around and just watched us, and I was so proud. Then we got a little clap and they all got up."

Jane smiles. "He swept Vi off her feet – twice."

Although Jane saw a lot of Vi throughout her childhood, it wasn't until she grew up and moved to Auckland that they really became close. Jane, who handles media liaison for the All Blacks, is best known to New Zealanders as a television sports journalist, most notably covering yachting, including two America's Cup campaigns. From the earliest days in her career, her grandmother has been an important source of support and encouragement. "I think your grandparents are a step enough removed for you to get closer in some ways than you can to your parents when you are younger."

When Jane first started work in television Vi was delighted, but constantly frustrated at not being able to see Jane's face.

"In those days you didn't do a lot of pieces to camera," explains Jane. "There was a feeling that if you were always showing up on camera you were pushing yourself. But boy did I get an earful. 'Why can't we see you? Why can't you show your face?'"

Although she looks back on those early days and cringes at her performance, Jane never heard a word of criticism from her grandmother.

"She's totally biased. Thank God for that. It was bloody awful. She's loyal-to-the-bitter-end-fan-club. That's the fantastic thing about grandmothers. You can't do anything wrong. With both my grandmothers I was not able to be criticised – these guys were totally biased."

Jane's passion for sport may well be in her genes, if her grandmother is anything to go by. While Jane is well aware that Vi loves to watch sport and competed in basketball as a youngster, she is surprised when her grandmother pulls out a series of newspaper clippings.

"I treasure these, they are very old," Vi says, carefully unfolding one clipping from the *New Zealand Sporting and Dramatic Review* dated November 17, 1927. "This is Carlaw Park. I played inter-house sports there in my teens, many years ago. That's me at the hurdles. I wasn't trained to be in the hurdles. I stayed too much in the air. I'm in the Girls' Brigade here, fourth one down."

Jane is fascinated. "The one with the good legs! You've never shown me these. The things you learn."

Vi points out another photo, this time of the hoop team where she and her team mates are dressed in smart sports frocks (red and gold), stockings and white shoes. "We used to jump through hoops, run around to the front, jump through again and step back."

That passion for sport has never faded.

"Whenever I ring up and there's cricket on, it's, 'Didn't you know the cricket was on? Aren't you watching it?'" says Jane.

The pair often discuss rugby matches and with the advent of pay-TV and the Super 12 competition, Jane arranged a Sky subscription for Vi to make sure she didn't miss any important games.

They often just visit each other for a chat, and occasionally go shopping or drive to Ngahinepouri to see Jane's parents.

Jane has found that those long drives an ideal opportunity for her to find out more about her grandmother. "In the last drive back to Auckland we talked about her father and that was, I think, quite hard. It's 75 years since he died and still she can remember it like yesterday and the impact that it had on her life. She was 15 and had to leave school and work to help her family. It just makes me feel so humble and lucky with the life that I have had."

So where does Vi get her strength from? After initially laughing off the question, Vi squirms and replies, "I don't know – other people go through the same. I'm not anyone special."

Jane: "You are."

Vi: "No I'm not – you make me feel as though I am, I don't know why.

Jane: "Well you are."

Vi: "If I am, give me another biscuit."

Jane spreads another biscuit and the two of them settle into the couch together to watch the game.

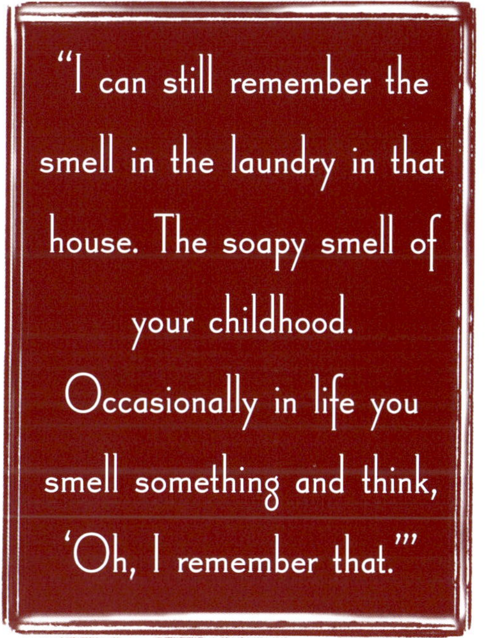

Piripi Cope &
his grandson Tamahou

Piripi Cope is a natural story teller and comedian, used to keeping people entertained in his role as kaumatua [elder] and informal historian in the village of Taheke in Northland's Hokianga.

However, when he talks about his hopes for Tamahou, his mokopuna atawhai [adopted grandson] his eyes fill with tears and he's uncharacteristically lost for words – for about five seconds.

"He's my life," Piripi says of the 14-year-old. "I have devoted all my time into him – not for any ulterior motive except to make life a better place for him. I can only do so much for him in the end. It's going to be up to him and I have to accept whatever it is going to be."

Tamahou has lived with the man he calls Papa since he was born and in all that time has never spoken a single sentence of English to Piripi, choosing to stick to their first language, Maori.

"His father asked me to teach him Maori and so I did," says Piripi, a former teacher with qualifications in bilingual teaching. "If you compare him with a monolingual child of the same age he has twice as many words in his head because he has two languages to draw from. His reading skills were all done in Maori first and when he was 10 he switched over to total immersion English. In 18 months he was up to his chronological reading age in English and he'd never read English in his life before."

And the advantages of having Maori as a first language? "At the end of the day for me and for him it's not going to be his English side that is going to put him at rest," says Piripi. "We have many part-Maori people in this world who have been brought up monolingually and they want to die Maori, but there is nothing to take them back to that Maori language or Maori side of them."

Tamahou and Piripi's journey together began with Tamahou's father, Peter, who was a student at a Wellington school Piripi was teaching at many years ago.

"He used to come and mow my and my flatmate's lawn and suddenly he didn't want to go home any more. He came from a big family of 13 children and ended up

staying and his parents were quite happy," recalls Piripi.

Peter came and went from Piripi's house and eventually moved back in with his partner, June, when the couple were in their early 20s and expecting their first child. Piripi was there the night the baby was born. "I picked him up when he was about five minutes old and I think that time was very special and some bonding happened," he recalls.

The child was named Tamahou, the name of Piripi's grand-uncle from Taheke.

"So we had our baby," he smiles.

A remarkable thing happened in those early weeks of Tamahou's life: Piripi always seemed to hear Tamahou in the night while the child's parents, who were in the same room as the baby, slept through his cries. "I would go through, have him changed and fed and everything – he wouldn't take to the breast so he was easy in terms of bottle feeding – and they wouldn't hear a thing," says Piripi.

Three months after Tamahou's birth, Piripi went to Rarotonga and the child fretted for him. It was a sign of things to come. Fourteen months after Tamahou's birth, Piripi left Wellington to return to the Far North to teach and the child was devastated.

"I was home here about eight days and Peter rang me and said, 'Dad, this boy's sick.'"

The child was in agony, covered in fluid-filled lumps the doctor thought were infected flea bites. Piripi, who was going to Auckland for a 21st party, arranged for a cousin in Wellington to bring the child to him in Auckland. He met them at the airport.

"They were the last people off the plane and when that door opened Tamahou saw me and… " He breaks off, demonstrating the child's delighted face, arms wide open – "He hugged me. We took him home that night and after he had had tea and we put him down to bed to sing and read to him he fell off to sleep."

But within 20 minutes the child was awake and screaming. "He looked and saw me and grabbed me and held me and it was the most heart-wrenching thing," says Piripi. "So I was walking around in my sister's house, my mother was crying, my sister was crying, I was crying and I was singing to him and the next day all those sores were gone. He had been totally stressed."

Blinking away his tears at the memory, Piripi recalls that after a few happy days together Tamahou returned to Wellington. This time Peter's call came within five days. "He said, 'Dad, you'd better come and get this boy. He's sick, he's screaming and he gets off the bed in the middle of the night and he's calling, 'Papa, Papa!'"

Piripi knew at that moment an important decision would have to be made about the child's future. "I said, 'Boy, you realise if I come and get him I'm coming to get him for good?' and he said, 'Yeah Dad.'"

Tamahou's parents had talked about the prospect of Piripi adopting the child and, although miserable at the thought of being parted from him, feared for his health if he was to stay separated from his papa.

"I was on a plane the next night and back here with my baby on Saturday ready to start being principal of a new school!" grins Piripi, who soon rallied support in the form of baby-sitting services from the local community.

Tamahou, now a shy, quietly spoken adolescent, still carries some memories of those days. "I remember one time when I was in Wellington, I think, I was a little baby and he went somewhere and I started crying for him at the door. I can remember it like I was watching myself crying and crying," he says.

A couple of months after Tamahou moved to Northland, his parents arrived for an Easter visit. "It was really lovely and right up to the time they left, if they had said they were going to take him, I would never have stopped them, but just before they went, his mother came up and said, 'Here you are Dad' and handed him over and they were happy," says Piripi. "I think their second child was conceived at my place if I've got my dates right!"

Later on that year Piripi and Tamahou flew to Wellington for June's father's tangi [funeral] and Piripi introduced himself to her family. "One of the kaumatua stood up and went through all the connections of the parents to Ngapuhi [Piripi's tribe] and he said, 'He is yours.' So he was given to me by her people and that's why I have never legally adopted him because for me it was a customary adoption. They gave me that child. Her people did."

Piripi takes seriously his responsibility to pass on the child's whakapapa [genealogy] from his Ngati Porou and Ngati Toa side as well as his adopted Ngapuhi side from Northland.

He's unabashed about his high expectations for Tamahou. The boy, a skilled artist who has drawn from an early age, is growing up in an area renowned for high unemployment and serious drug problems. It's an area which Piripi readily acknowledges doesn't offer a lot of hope for its young people. But Piripi is determined Tamahou is going to succeed. He set up an education fund for the child when he was five months old and expects that Tamahou will have a university education.

"I don't care how poorly he behaves because the reality is he is going to succeed. There is no option about it. I think that's where a lot of Maori people go wrong because they don't have the aspirations for their children.

"His mates drink alcohol and smoke and he can't stand it and so, even though I have a sneaky cigarette and a sneaky beer, I never do that in front of him because it's a whole role modelling thing. When he's older he can make his own decisions."

Piripi, who these days works as a kaiwhakarite [service broker] for Te Puni Kokiri – and in his spare time is a talented music composer – has tried to teach the child "traditional values" about being humble and

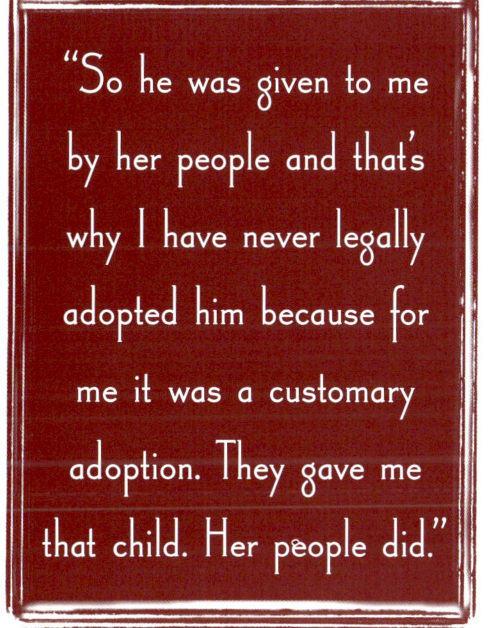

not bringing disrepute on the family.

So far, he's delighted at the way the boy has turned out. "He has never asked for anything. He has never been demanding because he has been given everything he needs and most of what he wants. He's an exceptionally capable rugby player. He's an obedient child. He's a nice person. He's very helpful, very cooperative and he's independent. He can clean, he can cook, he can wash his own clothes."

Of course there have been hiccups in Tamahou's exemplary behaviour. Piripi noticed recently that the boy had started to tattoo his own shoulder. Fearing that he would end up disfiguring himself in the same way as his friends who were covered with "ugly tattoos", Piripi decided to "manage the situation".

Not long afterwards, his cousin, a talented tattooist, arrived unexpectedly with a Dutch researcher in tow who wanted to pick Piripi's brain about the area's history. The timing couldn't have been better.

"I asked him if he would do a tamoko on Tamahou and he agreed and then we asked Tamahou, and he said yes. It took some 10 minutes before he agreed."

The tattooist drew up a design for Tamahou's shoulder and went to work. "Just before he started we did the karakia [prayers] and one of my cousins was here as well and we sang traditional waiata [songs] and it didn't hurt, did it Tamahou? Not really."

Tamahou eyes his grandfather. "When it first started it was sore but when he kept doing it, it wasn't that bad."

The pair do agree that the experience was deeply emotional. The tattoo serves several purposes. It is an attractive design of which Tamahou is proud, it covers the tattoo he started himself and it acts as a deterrent to stop him disfiguring himself in future.

"My cousin Gordon said to him, 'You will not ever touch yourself again. If anybody is going to do any more I am.' So he has been absolutely forbidden," says Piripi.

Grinning, his grandson Tamahou acknowledges that there's no chance of that. What's more, his tattoo is the envy of his friends. "When my mates saw mine they wanted to get one."

Piripi believes this approach to "reading the situation and thinking ahead" is the most effective way to raise children. "I really believe that the wairua, the spirituality, was right. The timing was right. The tattoo has given him mana – it's a blessing."

The following was written for Tamahou when he was four years old:

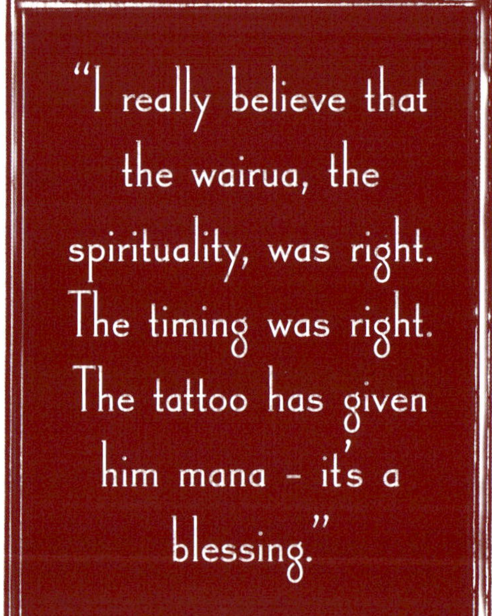

Ki Taku Mokopuna

E tama, ko tenei to ao
Na nga atua i hanga
Na o tupuna i tiaki
Na o matua i hoatu
Ki a koe e tama.

Anei te whenua, ko te aha koe?
Kua kitea e koe nga mea huna
Ma te mahi a ou ringa ka puawai
Ma te ahuwhenua ka whai hua
E tama, ko tenei to ao.

Maka atu to kupenga e tama
He aha nga mea i hopukina ai?
He kai? Whakawhetai atu ki a ratou ma
Tohatoha atu ki to whanau
Ko tenei to whakaakoranga
E tama, ko tenei to ao.

Titiro atu ki te pae o te rangi
Puritia nga mea kei mua i a koe
Ko te matauranga, hei aha?
Hei whakapai i tou ao
Kaua e tukua kia ngaro ai
E tama, ko tenei to ao.

I whanau mai koe, he Maori
Ka mate ra koe, he Maori
Whakaarohia e tama
Ko te roa o tou oranga, he Maori koe
Maumahartia ki oku korero nei
E tama, ko tenei to ao.

Na Piripi Cope

To My Grandson

My boy, this is your world
The gods have created it
Your ancestors have cherished it
Your parents have handed it
To you, my boy.

Here is the land, what will you do with it?
You have seen the hidden potential
By the skill of your hands it will blossom
By the toil of work it will bear fruit
My boy, this is your world.

Cast out your net, my boy
What are things that you have caught?
Is it food? Give thanks to them
Distribute amongst your family
This is your teaching
My boy, this is your world.

Look unto the horizon
Hold on to those things in front of you
Like education, what is it for?
It is to enrich your world
Don't let it be lost
My boy, this is your world.

You were born a Maori
You will die a Maori
Just think my boy
For as long as you live you are Maori
Always remember my words
My boy, this is your world.

Translation by Piripi Cope

Gamel O'Brien & her three grandmothers: Nana Mary O'Brien, Granny Marie Grünke & Grandma Jenny Lynch-Blosse

When Oamaru five-year-old Gamel O'Brien is in need of some grandmotherly advice, she is spoiled for choice.

She can pop into the second-hand book store in Oamaru's historic precinct to see her Grandma Jenny, she can scoot two doors down to the book bindery to see her Granny Grünke, she can wander up the road to see Nana O'Brien, or she can wait until Friday afternoon and head down to the Criterion corner bar to see all three.

Having three grandmothers is completely normal for Gamel, one of a growing number of children for whom open adoption laws have created a more complex extended family. Except in Gamel's case, it's not she who is adopted, but her father. Gamel is the only child of Oamaru couple Kahren Thompson and Michael O'Brien. Grandma Jenny is Kahren's mother Jenny Lynch-Blosse; Granny Grünke is Michael's birth mother Marie Grünke, and Nana O'Brien is Michael's mum Mary O'Brien.

Sitting now in the historic Criterion bar, five-year-old Gamel draws on five years of life experience in an effort to sum up what is special about each of them. At this point in her life it all comes down to what's on the menu.

Giggling, she says she likes to play tricks on Grandma Jenny, turning her boiled egg upside down when she's finished it to pretend she hasn't started. She also likes the "special puddings" at Jenny's place.

Nana O'Brien? "She reads me stories and cooks me noodles and eggs and sausages."

And guess what's special about Granny Grünke? "I like her house because sometimes I have jellies for breakfast. I like having jelly because it's nice and wobbly."

Gamel is too young to appreciate it just yet, but these three women are about as diverse as it is possible for three New Zealand grandmothers to be.

Nana O'Brien, at almost 80, is the eldest, a widow who lives the quietest life of the trio. Granny Grünke, 60, is a politically active, plainclothes nun who lives in a tiny stone cottage without electricity and works with her son in his book bindery. Grandma Jenny, also 60, is a former Auckland career woman who now runs the second-hand book store with her daughter and is active on the civic trust which oversees Oamaru's precious historic area.

The story of how these three women's lives became inextricably linked goes back to 1963 when Marie gave birth to Michael. Unwed and without church or government support, she felt she had no choice but to adopt out her child, an experience she found so traumatising she sought solace in spirituality, joining a convent in Australia.

Mary O'Brien entered the picture a couple of weeks after Michael's birth when she and her husband, John (who died in 1985), adopted the boy. Jenny Lynch-Blosse and her husband, Gerald, became part of the family when Jenny's daughter Kahren and Michael married.

The following year all their lives were turned upside down when Michael and Marie found each other and formed an instant bond. At the time Michael was still developing his reputation for great talent in the art of bookbinding and he and Kahren were beginning to reject the life of modern Auckland. Marie was also exploring the options for a self-sufficient lifestyle. Eventually, their mutual desire to live a more simple life took Michael, Kahren and Marie to Oamaru, a once-thriving port town, which still has a few pristine streets of ornate stone buildings left over from the Victorian era.

Kahren's mother, Jenny, and her husband, Gerald, joined them, much to their own surprise, when they went to Oamaru to look at a property Michael and Kahren wanted to buy and ended up falling in love with the place. Mary followed soon after. "When the family came down here and I was left all by myself up in Whangarei, I had phone calls just about every second night saying, 'Mum you've got to come down here – everybody else is here.'"

Jenny smiles at her granddaughter. "We've looked after Gamel since she was a baby. She's always come and stayed with us – sometimes just so Kahren and Michael could do their own thing and have time for themselves."

Mary has also found it rewarding to be at close quarters to her only grandchild. "In lots of ways I can see her daddy as I saw him when he was her age and that brings back memories for me of Michael. It's the way she looks at me sometimes, the mischievous grin because she's always having me on. In lots of ways she's very like her dad and of course seeing her growing up it's very important."

However, for Marie, her delight in watching Gamel grow up is tinged with other emotions.

"Sometimes I have moments, when I'm with Gamel, of deep sadness because it's reminding me of what I didn't have with Michael. I'll be in the playground and she wants

Gamel O'Brien with her three grandmothers: (left to right) Grandma Jenny, Nana O'Brien and Granny Grünke.

to feed the ducks or have a swing and I watch her running, playing, and I feel this real sadness come over me. And yet it's wonderful. I'm with her and I love her very much but it reminds me of what I didn't get with Michael."

She is careful to stress that the sadness is not a negative thing. "It puts you in touch with your grief, so naturally that is also very healing. Gamel in her own way is helping me really to heal a lot of the scars and deep wounds around just a tragic loss."

Marie is also clear about the fact that Gamel is no substitute for the child she didn't have the chance to raise. "You can never replace that loss. I thought for a while that could happen, but it's not like that. Nobody can replace what you've lost, but she's a wonderful healing presence in my life. I wouldn't like that to sound like a heavy responsibility on her shoulders. I don't think she's even aware of it. It's just a fact that I'm aware of."

While their backgrounds may be very different, all three grandmothers have growing common interests, and gather regularly as a family. Both Jenny and Marie are active in the local historic area and dress in Victorian clothing for work and historic area occasions. They're delighted that Gamel, who wears modern clothes to school, enjoys dressing in "trad" style when she's with them.

"She loves dressing up!" says Marie. "She goes around town looking at people saying, 'They're not trad, Gran!'"

As the three women sit around the table in the Criterion snug, chatting with Gamel about her day at school, it's clear this child will never be short of love. As far as they're concerned, Gamel is triple-blessed.

"In the old tradition the grandmothers were very important because they were the keepers of the stories," says Marie. "In this case Nana is the only living person with stories of Michael when he was little and she has those stories for Gamel. Grandma has stories of Kahren and the extended family for her, and I have the stories of the extended family on the genetic side too. Between the three of us we are all in a way irreplaceable."

Tim Woon
& his granddaughter
Greer Lindsay

Standing almost 2 m tall, Tim Woon has always been a dapper figure on the golf course. In his heyday, between 1950 and 1955, Tim took the New Zealand amateur golfing championship title four times without having had a single golf lesson.

Almost half a century later, aged 77, he's lost only a couple of centimetres to gravity and still gets the same kick out of the sport, especially now he can potter around his local, the Mount Maunganui Golf Course, with his golden-haired granddaughter in tow.

Greer Lindsay, who pays weekend and holiday visits from her home in Auckland, was only two-and-a-half when this photo was taken, but her grandad can already see potential in the child.

"She's a determined little kid, that one there. She'll have a go at anything. She has good ball sense. Even when she couldn't walk I remember her sitting there on her bottom with a ball, trying to scoop it up with a plastic club, then she gave it a clip."

As a birthday treat Tim had a professional five iron club cut down to Greer's size. "It's a bit heavy for her, but it's a good length and she'll grow into that."

But he'd be the last person on earth to put any pressure on the child to pursue golf seriously. "They must never be pushed into it. They lose interest and this is what I've seen with so many. How Tiger Woods did so well with his father obviously breathing down his neck all the time I don't know."

Whatever Greer decides to do in life, Tim believes her determination will get her there. "The other day she was sitting down there and she said, 'Don't talk to me Grandad when I'm reading.' She's old-fashioned. She's an old-timer that one."

As for Greer, she has just one thing to say about her grandad. "He's a good grandad because he loves me."

Dr Peter Sew Hoy
& his grandmother Fanny

There are few people in Dr Peter Sew Hoy's life more cherished than his grandmother Mrs Fanny Sew Hoy. At 96, she's the oldest member of one of Otago's most prominent Chinese families, who can trace their lineage back to the 1860s gold rush.

Yet you won't ever see Peter, 40, greet his grandmother with a hug and kiss the way he does with his children. Instead, the pair exchange a handshake and a few warm words in Cantonese – the way grandparents and grandchildren have been doing in China for centuries. "It's not that we are not affectionate, we just don't show it physically," he explains

Moving between eastern and western customs comes as naturally as breathing to Peter, who was born, raised, educated and has lived his entire life in Dunedin. "I do what's appropriate in the situation. It's just automatic."

Growing up in 1960s New Zealand, Peter's childhood was neatly divided into two worlds: the slice of China that lay behind the doors of his home and his grandparents' home next door, and the New Zealand way of life outside. "We had two lives: our English life and our Chinese life," he says.

Peter remains strongly connected to his cultural heritage – something he puts down to his close relationship with Fanny and her husband, Hugh, who died in 1997.

"We are very traditional. We call all the great-uncles and great-aunts by their correct titles. It's because of Grandma and Grandad that I know so much tradition and know and speak Chinese. My children maintain some of the Chinese. We've been fortunate in that we've had a lot of the family live to a great age; that and living so close to one another."

Some of Peter's earliest memories are of Fanny cooking up a storm in Dunedin's historic Sew Hoy building. "Ma [Chinese for paternal grandmother] cooked meals for her sons and extended family until she was well into her 80s."

That building is a rich part of the family history. It was originally owned by Peter's great-great-grandfather, Choie Sew Hoy, who ran his mercantile business there after arriving in Dunedin in 1868. Peter's grandfather Hugh (known in China as Choie Bak Pang) was Choie Sew Hoy's grandson, who grew up in China and originally came to New Zealand in 1920, intending to get an education. Instead he ended up working for his uncle in the family business. Three years later he returned to China to marry young Fanny (known then as Kong Yow Foon).

In 1938, Hugh returned to Dunedin, this time in a desperate attempt to arrange his family's immigration because the Japanese were threatening Southern China. But he was too late. Soon after he left, the Japanese invaded China and Fanny, pregnant with their sixth child, had to flee their Guangzhou home with the children. It would be nine long years before the family were reunited. In the meantime, Fanny was on the run from the Japanese.

"They were in groups of about 50, extended family," says Peter, translating for Fanny, who speaks only Cantonese. "Grandma can remember the Japanese war planes coming and she could hear the bombing, so it must have been close. There wasn't a lot of food. Grandma says they had to grow a lot of their own crops as they went. Her youngest boy was very sick and she remembers carrying him for long distances."

Speaking softly but clearly, Fanny sits ramrod straight in her chair, her hands resting on her knees one moment, then suddenly springing into action the next to punctuate her words. She recalls with absolute clarity, and without a trace of bitterness, the hardest nine years of her life.

"Grandma is saying if she had the chance she could write a book about it," says Peter. "This is what we should be doing while she is still alive and still has the memories of it."

When Fanny and the children were finally reunited with Hugh in Dunedin in 1947, the family adopted English names and set about negotiating life in a peaceful country with an alien language and culture. Twelve years later, with the help of his sons, Hugh established a clothing business which prospered, expanding into six clothing factories and employing hundreds of workers.

Fanny says she never considered returning to China. "The family had lost everything there anyway during the Japanese invasion. It was good here. The family was reunited, the business was doing well and it was very busy," translates Peter. "She worked until she was in her 80s."

For many years the whole extended family lived in the Sew Hoy building. Then Fanny and Hugh's children started moving out as they married and built their own houses.

"I lived in the building until I was five," says Peter. "It was the centre of the family. They used to have weddings there; they used to invite all the Chinese university students there for Sunday meals. It was the hub of the Chinese community."

But even when they moved into separate homes, the family stayed close. Peter has fond memories of the earliest days of television when he used to sit on his grandmother's knee and she would gently scratch his back as they watched the small screen. He recalls the way she has always marked birthdays, anniversaries and achievements in the traditional Chinese way, by handing over a "red packet," a small, decorated red envelope with money tucked inside.

One of the reasons Peter feels particularly close to his grandmother is the way she stepped in to help when his mother died of breast cancer at the age of 40.

"I was in my first year at university and Grandma and

Grandad were like parents to my brother and sister and myself. We lived next door and after Mum passed away they cooked meals for us and wanted us to come over and stay, and really they took over that responsibility. Dad was really lost at that time obviously.

"After Mum died we knew we had that stability. We knew that Grandma cared. We had Grandma and Grandad and we never wanted for anything. I can't think of having better grandparents when I look back."

Fanny too remembers those difficult years and how worried she and her husband were about the effect of his mother's death.

"I was doing my medical intermediate year," explains Peter, who has been a general practitioner since 1984. "My grandad was really worried about how I'd do, especially because Mum had just passed away, and they were so proud when I got four As and got into medical school. That's something she remembers."

Fanny Sew Hoy has always encouraged her 27 grandchildren (and now 44 great-grandchildren) to "study hard, be good at everything, be a good citizen".

So she is paying Peter a high compliment when she speaks of his intelligence, diligence and responsibility.

"She thinks I have taught my children a lot of the values that she thinks are important."

But, curiously, in some aspects of Chinese culture, Peter is the more traditional of the pair. For instance, he assumed that his grandmother would have strong feelings about family members marrying non-Chinese, but is surprised at her response.

"That's interesting. She says that it's okay as long as the couple is happy. I'm sure that 10 or 20 years ago she would have thought differently. I think with time, she's probably changed her viewpoint and become more open-minded. She says at the end of the day it's more important for the couple to be happy."

Seven years ago, a major blow struck the Sew Hoy family when the Sew Hoy & Sons clothing business fell prey to changing economic times, which meant the removal of import tariffs and a wave of cheap imports coming into New Zealand.

"The family lost face when the business went down because we had been here so long; we had employed so many people," says Peter. "There was no wrongdoing on our part. It was the economy at the time, but we are very proud people and it hurt a lot. Grandad especially. But people here know what the family has done. I have patients who used to work for the company and they have a lot of respect for Grandma and Grandad."

The business could not be saved, but Peter and his brother and sister stepped in and bought the Sew Hoy building when the business collapsed. "That's our heritage," Peter says.

That heritage is something he is at great pains to protect, through his personal efforts to teach his children all about their Chinese past and his more public efforts as chairman of the Otago Southland Chinese Association. Peter plans to record his family's fascinating history and is well aware that most of the story lies within the memory of his grandmother.

"She can remember so much, so much history. I don't want it lost. I want it to be recorded. My family had a very significant role to play in Otago and I'm very proud of it and I would like to see the family acknowledged."

Eva Greenfield & her granddaughter Louise

Twenty years ago, Louise Greenfield could always count on her grandmother for some kind words and a gentle rub if she fell over and hurt herself. Nowadays, it's Louise, a physiotherapist, who gently rubs away Eva Greenfield's aches and pains.

But don't imagine there's been a complete role reversal. On the eve of her 90th birthday, Eva is still on call for grandmotherly advice and affection.

"Nana is such a special lady. She's always been a real listening ear," smiles Louise. "I can always talk to her when I need a bit of wise counsel.

"She's always been there for the down times, with various romance break-ups, that kind of thing. Nana has always been the one to cry on and to pray with and to hug. We're both Christians and the church is a big part of us, so we can pray together or read the *Bible* or go to church together."

Something that has never changed between the couple is Louise's fascination with her grandmother's stories, and with a life spanning the best part of the 20th century, Eva has some good yarns to tell such as her experiences of the 1931 Napier earthquake. At the time Eva was newly married and living on a farm near Hastings.

"We lost a lot of our wedding presents. The chimney came right down through the roof onto the floor, and in the bedroom the dressing table was whizzed right across the room and turned completely around."

Louise says, "There are all sorts of good stories. I have a cousin who is about the same age, and we would always have holidays with Nana and she would tell us stories – not so much historical stories but more moral stories."

Eva laughs. "We had the two, Janice and Louise, and this one was always perhaps a bit more impatient than Janice. The two of them would get into bed with me and I'd drop off to sleep and they'd say, 'Wake up Nana – you haven't finished the story!'"

These days the pair live in the same part of Auckland and Louise tries to see her grandmother every couple of weeks. "We usually have a meal together or a drink, or sit out in the conservatory and have a chat. Occasionally we go for a walk along the waterfront, or I give Nana a bit of a rub."

Eva nods, "We are just a very quiet couple."

Alison Holst
& her granddaughters
Elizabeth & Jennifer Holst Buxton

It could be argued that Alison Holst plays a grandmotherly role in the lives of thousands of New Zealanders. As well as the screeds of original recipes she has dreamed up in almost 40 years as a food writer, Alison has recipes for the basics we forgot to ask our own grandmothers to write down.

Without a hint of condescension, she'll spell out how to make stuffing, or which way up to roast a chicken, adding a few gems of advice to ensure the recipes are economical both in time and money – an approach that would earn any grandmother's nod of approval. But get her onto the subject of what it was like to become a real grandmother and that familiar calm, patient voice falters just a little as she tries to explain it.

"I just couldn't believe this was my baby's baby," she murmurs, her voice still full of wonder. "It was quite overwhelming, astounding."

Her baby's baby is Elizabeth Margaret Holst Buxton, born in 1985 to Alison and Peter's daughter Kirsten.

"She came home with this precious baby every holiday, and we all shared the baby and had the most wonderful time with it, which is something I will never forget," says Alison. "She is a very special little girl."

Alison now has three grandchildren: Elizabeth, 14, and her seven-year-old sister Jennifer, to Kirsten and husband Mark, and baby Isabella, to son Simon and his wife, Sam (who were expecting their second child as this book went to press).

"Grandma Holst" takes a traditional approach to grandmotherhood, using many of the hours she spends with the children to gently school them in skills which use their hands as well as their brains.

"I think that the role of grandparent is really important, especially when you have young, professional, working parents who have enormous demands with their work," she says. "It's cooking and sewing and little things like making your bed and tidying the bedroom and turning it into a game, which you don't have time to do when you are rushing off to work… just teaching useful things which improve the quality of their lives. I hope my grandchildren will remember that they've done some special, and some funny things with me."

For Elizabeth and Jennifer, who spend a large chunk of their school holidays at Alison's Wellington home, or the family beach-house at Manakau, the days are packed with projects – cross-stitching or embroidering presents for each other, making teddy bears, learning to cook family recipes, making pictures with rubber stamps – as well as reading piles of books and going for long walks.

Alison, who is still "enormously busy", makes every effort to clear her commitments when her grandchildren are staying.

"As far as I'm concerned, you must make time for your family because they are children for such a short time.

Elizabeth is now 14 and when she asked if we could have a family picnic to celebrate her birthday, I was quite surprised that this was what she wanted to do. Next year she'll probably want to do something with her peers.

"I am lucky because I'm self-employed, so I can usually make time to do things with the children."

One of the reasons it's so important for Alison to make time for the grandchildren is the great support she had from her own mother when she was busy working and raising a family.

"Kirsten was very close to my mother and when I hear her talking I can still hear many of my mother's phrases. Kirsten will sometimes make me something that she and my mother used to cook together, or she will make Peter a batch of rock cakes that his mother made for him. It's so special when somebody thinks about such things. It really takes me back. I hope that Elizabeth and Jennifer will do exactly the same thing in years to come. It's very important to pass on special skills."

During the last couple of school holidays, Elizabeth has been helping Alison test recipes for two cookbooks.

"She did a very good job. She regarded it very seriously, as she should have, and she now uses the first book with great pride.'"

Elizabeth says the experience of cooking meals was a

> "Now with your grandchildren, your children are doing those vital things and you are there for the fun. You get the good bits."

lot more difficult than she'd imagined. "It was really cool, but it's so hard organising the different parts of a meal. It's hard work. I don't want to have to cook for my family when I'm older!"

Alison hopes the exercise was useful for her granddaughter. "I've said to her, 'Well now you can make [these things]. If someone is having a birthday and you want to give them something and you don't have the money, you can make them a batch of cookies or fudge'. These are life skills I think grandparents should be there to help with. I hope that she will be able to look at those books and introduce her children to cooking and remember that we worked on those recipes together."

But it's not just practical skills Alison passes on to the children. She's also there as a wise confidante when they need someone to talk to.

"I think I can talk about some things with the children in a less confrontational way than a parent can. Elizabeth and I can discuss quite difficult issues in a way that is comfortable to both of us, where it may not always be like that with a parent, who's much closer. To be able to stand back a little bit is great. It's one of the really wonderful things about being a grandparent."

Elizabeth agrees. "We've always talked to each other and I've never had a problem talking to Grandma."

Alison laughingly acknowledges that her relationship with her teenage granddaughter is far easier than it was with her own teenage children.

"As a parent your job is different. You have to teach so many important things. It's a responsibility… Now with your grandchildren, your children are doing those vital things and you are there for the fun. You get the good bits. It's not that you don't reinforce what parents say and do, especially if you've received a whispered message that there are a few problems. You are working with parents, not against them.

"Elizabeth said something recently that summed it all up. She said, 'We're all friends in our family. We are not just relations' and I thought that was a very special thing for a 13-year-old to say."

Not, she adds, that they don't drive each other up the wall every now and again. "Every different generation must have their moments with each other. I'm sure there are times when we drive the girls crazy and they drive us mad, but we can laugh about it a short time later."

Another critical difference Alison has noticed between her grandchildren and children is that her grandchildren are more relaxed about her public profile. While her children, as teenagers, would practically "put on balaclavas" so they were unrecognisable when forced to go out in public with her, the grandchildren have no problem with it.

"It's absolutely acceptable in a grandmother. Elizabeth couldn't care a bit."

Elizabeth agrees. "She's really normal. She is a normal sort of grandmother. She doesn't do work when we are around – only when she really has to – and then she organises stuff for us to do. She's really nice and doesn't treat us like little kids. It's always fun to go and stay with them and see them. It's not like a chore or anything."

Jennifer, too, reckons it's good fun at Grandma Holst's house.

"She makes yummy desserts – banana splits."

Asha Osman & her granddaughter Fatima

Fatima Osman's face relaxes into an expression of wonder as her grandmother Asha gathers up her vibrant robes, nestles into her favourite sofa and starts telling stories.

Asha is talking about her home country, Somalia, but for a New Zealand-born child like Fatima the place she is describing is as strange as a fairy-tale world.

Although well aware Fatima is destined to grow up a New Zealander, Asha is determined that will not happen at the expense of the child's Somali culture.

"English will be easy for the grandchildren because they are living in New Zealand," Asha says, speaking through an interpreter. "But more important is the culture and the values, where they're from, where we came from and how we grew up over there.

"A grandparent holds first place for the children in Somalia," she explains, adding that in Somalia there is no concept of the nuclear family, which keeps many New Zealand grandparents at arm's length from their grandchildren. "Grandchildren are a new generation and we show them love and care for them and help them grow up the same way that we grew up."

One example of the differences between a Somali and a New Zealand upbringing is that Fatima won't learn household chores such as cooking, making beds, doing the laundry and cleaning until she is much older. "Children cannot cook until they are 13. They are not allowed to take responsibility until they are older," explains Asha.

Fatima is one of few children in New Zealand's refugee community who has a grandparent involved in her daily life. Many families who have settled here are separated from their grandparents by thousands of kilometres. At worst, the grandparents may have perished in war, famine or harsh living conditions. In Somalia the average life expectancy for a woman is 47, so, at the age of 60, Asha has lived to what is considered a ripe old age.

For Somalis, whose culture centres around the family, grandparents are seen as vital in helping to raise children because of the knowledge and support they provide. That support is even more crucial for people like Fatima's parents, Luul and her husband, Aden Ilmi, who settled in New Zealand in 1993. They have had to adjust to life in a foreign country while raising children without the support of an extended family.

Asha hopes one day things will improve in Somalia and she will be able to take her grandchildren back for a visit.

Jim Becker & his grandson Sean

It's lunchtime at Jim and Flo Becker's house. Three generations of Central Otago farmers, Jim, 83, Pete, 49, and Sean, 23, sit around the dinner table finishing off last night's roast. The curtains are drawn to keep out the glare of the late summer sun and the television in the lounge is keeping them up to date with the cricket test between New Zealand and South Africa.

"I was cook today, so it was cold mutton and spuds and peas," apologises Jim, rocketing between kitchen and dining table, clearing plates and preparing tea, and making no allowances for his painfully stiff hip.

Sean grins, explaining the absence of the "cook". "Nana and Mum are down in Dunedin checking out granddaughters-in-law. They're having lunch with my girlfriend and my brother's girlfriend as well."

A prospect that would mortify most men his age amuses Sean as much as it does his father and grandfather. But the Beckers are in even brighter spirits than usual today. It is a time of great excitement for the family with Sean due to fly to Canada next week to represent New Zealand in the World Curling Championships – skip of the first New Zealand team ever to make it into the world competition. Pete will join them in a support role.

Curling, for the uninitiated, is like bowling on ice. Curlers hurl heavy granite stones across the ice towards a target, their team mates racing ahead with special brooms to sweep the ice and help guide the stone to its target.

The sport is a major part of the family history – Pete is a self-confessed fanatic, who has curled all his life and is secretary-treasurer of the New Zealand Curling Association; Jim is an enthusiast who once led a New Zealand team to Scotland, and Jim's father, also a hill country farmer, was passionate about the sport.

"My father was a blacksmith and curling was the only

relaxation that he ever had really, other than going out on the hills and mountains shooting," recalls Jim.

No surprise, then, that Sean started learning to curl about the time he learned to walk. "We have an old dam out the back, about 45 yards long with a couple of sets of lights on it for curling at night," he says. "I remember as a kid my grandad, dad and uncle pushing me and my cousins up and down the stones on the ice when they were curling. They'd give us a push and we would go spinning down the ice. We used to love it, just crashing the stones together because they make a lot of noise and kids are into noise. It was a lot of fun on a cold, frosty day."

Curling is a supremely social sport which, for a century and a half, has helped relieve the isolation that bitterly cold Otago winters can bring.

"In the winter there might be four or five inches of snow lying around and once all the stock is fed nobody has anything to do, so you have half a day to spare and there will be a curling match called and away you go," says Sean.

He and his two brothers and sister grew up with their parents, Peter and Wendy, in the house up the hill from Jim and Flo, all part of the 2632 ha the Beckers own on the hills overlooking the Maniototo Plain. His grandparents' house has always been his second home.

"When we were kids they were always the first stop before the bus and on the way home, and Nana would have a wee plate of biscuits ready for us every day after school," Sean recalls, adding that his grandfather even played a part in helping develop his hand-eye coordination. "Grandad used to throw lollies to us all the time. We weren't allowed them unless we caught them, so we had to learn to catch fairly quickly!"

These days Sean works as a casual farm worker and lives in Gimmerburn, 20 minutes' drive from home, but he still sees a lot of his grandparents. He's often invited for dinner, or he'll turn up to watch a game of cricket or rugby or to do some work on the farm.

Jim is clearly proud of his grandson's achievements – more for the effort he's put in than the trophies and medals.

"He's stuck to it and that's what I like about Seany. There are not many young fellas that I know that have stuck with it like he has and carried it on. We are very proud of Seany, we really are."

Jim believes his grandson's laid-back attitude is the key to his success as a curler and the team skip – giving him the ability to keep his cool when the pressure is on.

Sean unhesitatingly explains that's all due to his upbringing. "Farming has a lot to do with that. You have to take the bad with the good."

Jim nods. "You have. Dead right."

There is an easiness between the two, an understanding that stems from years of spending long periods of time in each other's company. Over the years Jim has been a rich source of advice for Sean, mostly on the "farming side of things" but they've also talked a lot about the past, their family "pedigree" and Jim's war experiences.

"One thing about farm life," says Jim, "Sean and I could be working out in the shearing sheds or anywhere and it's not grandad and grandson. We are just cobbers. That's how it is, really, isn't it Sean? We are quite close and I am accepted by them as a knowledgeable bloke I suppose."

Jim chuckles at the thought but Sean agrees. "Yeah, experience counts for a lot."

Are there any particular values that Jim has taught his grandson? "I think there would be in lots of ways. We are pretty close and I think if you are close to each other you respect each other."

But Jim and Sean are well aware the clock is ticking on the close, regular contact between them. Opportunities are opening up all over the place for Sean, who has already travelled widely for curling training and competitions. If he decides to pursue the sport further he could become professional or train as a coach – both of which could take him overseas. He's also showing potential in rugby, reluctantly turning down a trip to Australia with the Otago Country side because he couldn't risk an injury in the build-up to the World Curling Championships. But already another attractive offer has emerged, this time from a French club side.

"I have to make a few big decisions with my life," he muses.

Then of course there is the option of one day taking over the family farm, but Sean is realistic about this one.

"I personally think that the days of the family farm are almost gone because the younger generation coming through don't necessarily want a farm. They have the technology to go places and do things. People from my generation tend to travel and do their OE and a lot of them don't come back.

"Dad has a lot of life left in him and until he retires… my brother and I will probably decide when it comes to that point, but I'm happy doing what I'm doing at the moment and curling has taken me a lot of places."

While some farmers of Jim's generation would be putting pressure on their grandchildren to commit to a future on the farm to keep it in the family name, Jim seems more interested in encouraging Sean to get the most out of life.

"I think, Sean, you are doing it the right way because the key is to go as far as you can in the sport and it will come to a day where it won't be so good for you, but then you might end up being a coach in Canada or Germany, anywhere. So there are doors open."

Whatever career move Sean makes and no matter where he sets up home, one thing is certain: he'll never be away from Patearoa for too long.

"I think the best thing is no matter what I do, I always have somewhere to come back to. I have a place you can call home. You can always come back and there will be people there that will support you no matter what happens. That's always good to have in the back of your mind. I think that helps me a lot with my curling too."

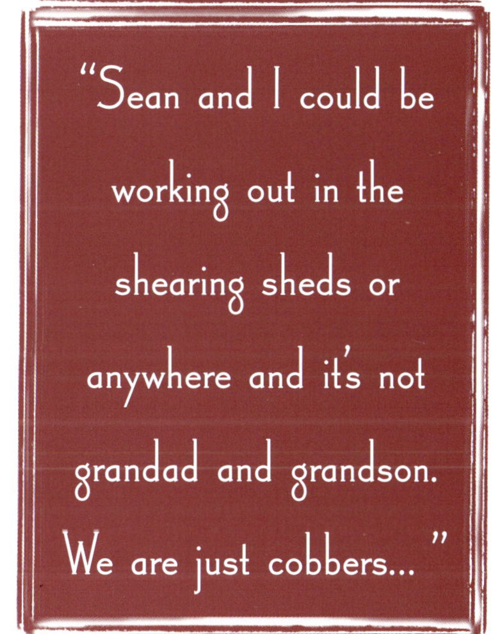

Tuti Tukaokao & his granddaughter Rita-Kay Tangataevaha

One day in the not too distant future Tauranga master carver Tuti Tukaokao will pick up a chisel and place it in the hand of his young granddaughter Rita-Kay. In that simple gesture, Tuti will both uphold and reject ancient Maori customs.

On one hand, he will be doing his duty to pass on the knowledge and skill of his ancestors, teaching his descendant to coax life out of wood and stone. On the other, he will break what was once a cardinal rule: Maori women must not carve.

But Tuti will be making no apologies. The precedent, he says, was set long ago. "You know the famous Guide Rangi from Whakarewarewa?" he asks. "Her grandfather taught her how to carve. There's also a meeting house up north carved by a woman. Now when I found that out I said, 'Who am I to say they can't learn to carve?'"

Tuti asked that question for the first time many years ago before starting his own carving school at Taumarunui, and eventually teaching carving at schools in the Bay of Plenty.

"Most of the students at the night classes were women," he says. "Nobody has ever got cross with me about it because when I tell them about Guide Rangi and that meeting house up north, they shut up."

He acknowledges that "in ancient times" women were banned outright from carving. "They weren't even allowed near a meeting house when it was being carved; they weren't even allowed to do the weaving – men did it all. But over the years women started doing some weaving and today most of the weaving is done by women. So things have changed for the better," he says firmly.

Tuti first learned to carve as an 18-year-old and within two years had started work on the ornate Tamatea Pokai Whenua meeting house at Huria on the inner reaches of Tauranga Harbour.

"I had just started a new job when our elders started to build the meeting house and they asked for 10 volunteers, so I chucked the job in and stayed home full-time. My grandmother said, 'That's OK, we can survive on my pension,' and that's how it was for six years. It was hard because our tutor came down six times in six years. There wasn't a full-time tutor like they have today."

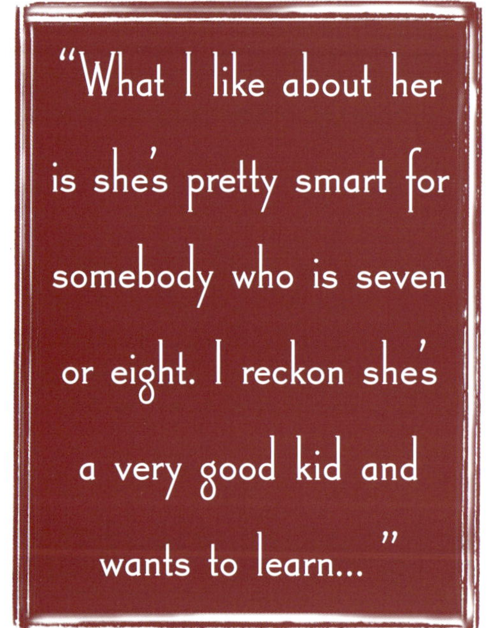

For inspiration, Tuti used to travel to Auckland when he could afford it to study the carving exhibits at the War Memorial Museum. He must have done something right, because the project was unveiled by the Maori King Koroki who was so impressed with Tuti's work he bestowed a rare blessing on the young carver. "He walked towards me and he embraced me and cried and, being young and fresh, I didn't know what was going on," Tuti recalls. "He put his hands on my shoulders and looked me straight in the eyes and said in Maori, 'Go forth and do the work of our ancestors. You are quite free to walk this land of the Tainui, the Waikato and King Country, and nothing will befall you,' and I have been under that protection ever since."

Over his 52-year career Tuti has carved seven meeting houses single-handedly and worked on more than 30. He's been involved in carving four waka (canoes) – one of which lies in a Polynesian village in Honolulu, and another at the Arts and Crafts Institute in Rotorua. One of his best-known carvings is the intricate wood panels lining the interior of the McDonald's restaurant in Rotorua. Tuti has also carved many stone sculptures using Hinuera, Mt Somers and Oamaru stone.

His tribal affiliations may resemble "a packet of

liquorice allsorts" but, as master carvers are expected to, he knows them all – right back to the canoes that brought the first Maori to Aotearoa.

"Tamatea was the captain of the Takitimu canoe. He had two wives and from the first wife comes our line and from the second wife comes the Maori King. On my grandfather's side, his mother was born in Rotorua and died in 1886 in the Tarawera eruptions. My grandfather was seven-and-a-half years at the time and he and his father and two sisters came back to Tauranga."

There are many more, such as the ancestor the Tukaokao family gets its name from – a brave warrior who was shot clean through the armpit at the battle of Gate Pa on April 29, 1864, and died seven days later.

Tuti even has an element of mystery in his own personal history. "Tuti is actually a nickname. My mother named me Duty and when I asked her why she just smiled and I waited for an answer. I said, 'It makes me feel like duty free!' Well, the smile got bigger but she never did give me an answer."

One possible clue might be the death of Tuti's two elder brothers in their childhood. "One fell off a tree at school and died; the other fell off the verandah at Grandad's house and broke his back after a dog leapt up on him. They were both called Tamatea. When I was born my grandfather called a meeting and told everyone that this name Tamatea was not to be used any more, but still people would call me Ta, short for Tamatea. My grandfather should have remembered 'third time lucky!'" he jokes. "I've had many accidents and scrapes and always come out of it!"

All this knowledge is a drop in the bucket compared to what Tuti is already beginning to pass on to his granddaughter Rita-Kay, who lives with her mum, Kathleen, in his house.

Sitting in his studio on the Tauranga waterfront, Tuti muses, "To me it's important to know your history, and carving is sacred amongst carvers, and I'm not talking about carvers who make souvenirs for tourists – they make a load of junk – and I cringe when I look at the souvenir shops. But Rita-Kay will know her tribal affiliations and genealogy and things pertaining to what the women do."

Already the child is showing a keen interest, happily sitting watching him carve for hours on end. But Tuti says she's too young to learn yet. "I don't know whether she'll want to carve. I won't encourage anybody to carve unless they really want to. I think she's more involved in sport and music, which is good, and also Te Reo Maori at school, which is helpful. What I like about her is she's pretty smart for somebody who is seven or eight. I reckon she's a very good kid and wants to learn. I went home one day and there she was on the computer, her fingers going flat out. I said to my daughter, 'Look at this child!' and she said, 'Dad, that's nothing.' It just blew me away."

While Tuti would love the child to become a carver, it's not an easy way to make a living and he wouldn't want her to learn at the expense of other skills which will help her secure a steady job and a bright future. "A lot of people can't get jobs and if you are in a position where you can be employed in the future, well you have to learn eh."

Chances are Rita-Kay will do both. She says she would like to carve a greenstone necklace one day, but is in no hurry. "At the moment Grandad doesn't show me how to carve. I just like watching."

Colin Meads & his 11 grandchildren

Even at 62 Colin Meads is a giant of a man both in stature and status as one of the greatest rugby players of all time.

But the man who represented New Zealand in more test matches than any other All Black of his time does everything he can to ensure his grandchildren don't grow up overwhelmed by his mighty shadow. He'd prefer them to remember him as a grandad who cared for them and "tried to point them in the right direction," rather than the man immortalised by a thousand photographs of him barrelling through the opposition in his Number Five jersey.

"I try to make it not important to them. I try to teach them to play as well as they can and achieve the best, but not everyone can be an All Black," he says simply.

His wife, Verna, 63, agrees. "We made a point when our own children were growing up that it was never a big deal. He went away to play rugby. That was all they were told. They were not aware he was an All Black. He had to be a father first."

But just as his own children were inevitably ribbed about their famous dad, his grandchildren are experiencing some of the same comparisons. There have been newspaper articles about the children's achievements, saying "grandson or granddaughter of Colin Meads".

"I think it's often a worry," says Colin. "I don't know that it's always fair. I think it doesn't tend to help them."

When photographed for this book, Colin and Verna had 11 grandchildren to their five children – with two more expected within a couple of months. The "townies" are Hayley, 13, Clinton, 11, and Kasie, four (to Karen), and Juliana, 11, Lara, nine, and Jacob, two (to Rhonda), who live in Hamilton. Little Baylee, 20 months, recently moved to Auckland with her mum, Shelley, who's also expecting another child. The grandchildren growing up in Te Kuiti are Hannah, nine, and Mitchell, six, who live with their dad, Kelvin, and Christy, five, and Abbe three, who live with dad, Glynn, on the old family farm.

Colin admits that when his first grandchild, Hayley, came along 13 years ago, she was a sharp reminder that he was getting on in years. "Nothing makes you age more than grandchildren!" he says with a laugh, admitting that the older they get, the more they make him feel his age.

But he has no complaints.

"I do enjoy being a grandfather. I enjoy it very much. The spice of life I call grandchildren. You don't have them all the time but when they are here you probably look after your grandchildren better than you looked after your own.

"It's probably because you have more time. When you are young – in my case we were very much into rugby whereas now we have more time."

Colin and Verna, who have a 243 ha sheep and beef farm near Te Kuiti, see a lot of their grandchildren. As well as big family gatherings every second Christmas, the local kids often stay with them when Verna and Colin are on baby-sitting duty. The Hamilton family tend to come to Te Kuiti for weekends and holidays.

"The ones from Hamilton – I suppose you'd call them the town kids – when they come here they want to be on the farm all the time helping you and doing things on the farm," says Colin. "They all pile onto the four-wheel motorbike with me and come out. The older ones are a big help on the farm and they help me drafting sheep or whatever we are doing at the time.

"They say they want to be farmers, but when you are that age … whether it's to impress grandad or grandma I don't know – but the days of farms being passed on from generation to generation are just about gone."

Colin says he's had to set down a few rules to ensure the town kids fit into country life – for instance, he won't have a bar of those city breakfasts.

"I'm a great one for the old hardy farmer eating a big breakfast. I set down rules. I say, 'You are only allowed to stay with Grandad if you eat a good breakfast.' So they all know that if they want to come and stay here they have to have sausages and eggs and potatoes."

What's more, it's Grandad who cooks it for them.

And do Colin's grandchildren understand the fact he's an All Black legend? "I think the older ones do now. The younger ones don't. It's just one of those things they learn as they grow up I suppose."

Colin is delighted that many of his grandchildren play sport, something he encourages wholeheartedly. "I just want them to enjoy their sport. It doesn't have to be rugby. Some of the children play rugby; the girls play netball, although the eldest one told us last year she was playing rugby at school now," he says with a smile.

He and Verna have been along to watch the children play in various matches and Colin is an enthusiastic but non-aggressive spectator. "I let them play their game and I don't force them. I just let them be themselves."

Overall, Colin regards being a grandparent as playing an "advisory role".

"Often as a grandparent you can sit down with them and talk about school and those sorts of things far easier than a parent can. I think the older grandchildren are confiding in us a lot more in the way of asking questions and that. It's nice that it's able to happen."

The values Colin and Verna attempt to instil in the children are straightforward. "I think the big thing is as long as they are active and healthy. We tend to encourage them to play sport and try and impress on them that they need an education these days."

Do they expect to stay close to their grandchildren? "Oh well that's one of the inevitable questions you can't really answer because you never know where life takes young people these days," says Colin. "Hopefully they'll always be coming back to their grandparents, put it that way."

Elizabeth Alexander & her grandson Alex Bromley

When Alex Bromley needs time out from his parents or baby sister he has a retreat shared by few New Zealand children these days - Grandma's room upstairs.

Elizabeth Alexander recently emigrated to Auckland from Devon, England, with Alex, four, and his family – his mum, Sally, dad, Richard (a New Zealander), and sister, Sophie, six months. Although Elizabeth's living arrangement is temporary, she says it has been a great experience living at close quarters with two of her grandchildren.

"Having the children is wonderful because one really doesn't have to discipline them in the way that I used to have to do with [my children]. I can spoil them or say, 'Go and see Mummy,'" the retired physiotherapist says. "I enjoy my time alone with Alex and Sophie when Mum and Dad aren't there because they are totally different. It's great fun."

A few moments later she's crawling about on the floor helping Alex make a train tunnel out of her favourite rug, showing no sign that she has two artifical hips.

Sally says Elizabeth's presence takes the weight off her shoulders. "When I'm in a rush and have lots and lots of things to do and then I hear Alex going, 'Oh Grandma,' Mum never says, 'Oh Alex, I'm just going to do this, I'm just going to do that.' She'll always stop and play with him.

"I look in and think, 'Great, Mum has him. That's wonderful.' He doesn't get that constant 'wait a minute.'"

Elizabeth's time spent with Alex usually revolves around playing games of all kinds or reading books. But she acknowledges there is a bigger picture to her role with the child. She hopes she can contribute to his upbringing in a way that complements what his parents are doing.

"I think one takes the guidance from Mum, then you try to bring them along and expand their views along the lines that Mum and Dad are taking."

Although Alex is still very young, his grandmother believes his thoughtful nature is already shining through.

"He looks after me. When the family is going out and I'm staying behind for peace and quiet, he gives me jobs to do so that I'm not lonely. He tries to find some job that I can do when he's away. And when he comes back he says to me, 'I've missed you'. Oh he's lovely."

Of course he's not an angel all the time. "Well he's shy at the moment, as you saw, but at other times when he's tired he's way over the top. He is, I suppose, a typical boy."

Marie Pilbrow & her granddaughter Hayley Thomas

Traditionally, it's the grandparents who provide a helping hand to their grandchildren, gently guiding toddlers to their feet, helping them prepare their meals and taking them to the shops or library.

But in the case of Christchurch 83-year-old Marie Pilbrow there's been something of a role reversal.

Marie has been blind for about 20 years since a series of haemorrhages caused permanent damage to her eyes. Although she's always maintained her independence, there are times Marie needs a little help and her grandchildren have grown up knowing just when to offer – especially her youngest granddaughter, Hayley, aged 15.

"Even when she was three she used to say, 'Nanny if you want to go to the toilet, I will take you.' Isn't that lovely?" laughs Marie. "She's sort of used to rescuing Nanny and taking her places."

As Hayley has grown up, she's been able to provide more and more practical support for her grandmother. "She writes my Christmas cards for me, wraps up my parcels and gets me things from the shops," says Marie. "She reads things to me that I can't read and she loves doing it."

It's also the little things the teenager does that Marie appreciates – for instance describing the food on the plate if she's passing around nibbles at a social occasion. "People sometimes just pass things around and they don't explain what is on the plate. The grandchildren are so used to explaining and describing things to me."

That skill is particularly useful during Hayley and Marie's shopping expeditions. "I just tell Nanny the colour and describe what it's like and she usually has a good idea of what she wants," says Hayley.

Marie describes all her grandchildren as "precious" but "Hayley is particularly special. She's the little one."

One of the reasons for the close bond between the pair is their profound love for animals. Hayley has always adored Marie's black Labrador guide dog Orissa and spends hours playing with the dog. Now she's mad on horses and in just one year of owning a horse has a roomful of ribbons for her

riding achievements at the local pony club.

"When Hayley was little she'd love taking Orissa outside and getting her to jump," laughs Marie who says Hayley's new hobby has provided a welcome opportunity to revisit her childhood passion for horses. "I was a country girl. I was brought up in North Canterbury in Horrelville near Rangiora and rode horses right from when I was four. We had little Shetland ponies and we always rode to primary school and we used to jump with them. They didn't have pony clubs like they do these days and so we used to ride in the local shows."

These days Marie has to leave Orissa at home when she heads down to the pony club when Hayley is competing (the dog would upset the horses) but she's willing to do without the dog's help for an hour or two just to be near the horses. "I love to go down to the pony club and cuddle the horses and talk to them and know all about them."

Another of her favourite pastimes with Hayley is playing games. "We play Braille scrabble together. We have a special board which the letters slot into and the edges of the letters are marked in Braille. Sometimes I have to ask Hayley exactly which way they are going and so forth," says Marie. "I don't think anyone ever wins. We don't have a winner do we Hayley? We just play for the fun of it."

While Marie doesn't dwell on her disability she points out that the one thing that consistently worries her about being blind is not being able to see her grandchildren. "I could see the older ones when they were little but the younger ones like Hayley, I haven't seen them grow up. I could do a lot more with the older ones but it's reversed now. They do look after me."

For many years after she lost her sight, Marie relied on "sighted guides", volunteers who helped her get around. But she found the experience humiliating. "People treated you like a zombie and they would always ask the sighted person, 'Does she want to sit down? Will she have a cup of tea or does she have sugar?' You just felt you had lost your identity."

It wasn't until the Foundation for the Blind provided her with a guide dog at the age of 75 that Marie felt like she had a fresh start in life. "I was the oldest person they had ever trained with guide dogs. So at 75 I found it wonderful to get back to independence. I am living in a retirement centre in my own cottage but I have my independence and I'll never give it up. The only thing I can't do for myself is the cleaning."

Marie says while some people have been rude or

insensitive over the years because they haven't known how to relate to someone who is blind, she's never had that experience with her grandchildren. In fact growing up around someone who is blind has made them generally a lot more understanding about people with disabilities.

Hayley says she has noticed she responds in a different way to disabled people than her friends do – especially at school where there are quite a few disabled students. "Some people just laugh at them and sort of think, 'That would never happen to me' but I don't think anything of it."

Hayley's mother, Annette, adds, "My children don't think anything of Mum being blind because they've grown up with it and it's just always been like that. It's never been a problem to them or something they've been embarrassed about. It's just their Nanny." While Marie is happy to share stories with Hayley about what life was like in the old days, she's doesn't like to dwell on the past with her grandchildren. "It is a very different world. We have to realise that it's a really different world. I think you have to grow up with your grandchildren. You can't expect them to do what we did. Life is very different. You have to live with the times and look at life through their eyes, don't you? You have to accept it or you get left behind."

There doesn't seem to be any risk of that, according to Hayley. "My friends say their grandparents are so old and don't know anything, but to me Nanny sort of doesn't seem like she's old."

Ihaka Pink
& his grandfather
David Garratt

I haka Pink hadn't even gasped his first lungful of air when his grandfather David Garratt wrote him his first letter. It was February 16, 1996, the day before Ihaka's birth, when David turned on his trusty laptop computer and tapped out a special blessing for the boy.

"I wanted to do something for Ihaka because he's our first grandchild," recalls David. "Even before he was born I felt like I wanted to influence him, not in a controlling way but with my wisdom, my understanding. I suppose I felt that grandparents have a unique opportunity to influence their grandchildren in a way that they don't really have even with their own children, because when you have your own children you are really learning all the time, you don't think in terms of how to impart wisdom."

That first letter welcomed Ihaka to the world, wished him the best in life and celebrated the six different races and cultures in his blood.

Since then, David has written many more letters to the boy who was almost three when this photograph was taken.

Although Ihaka is too young to understand the letters now David hopes that once he's a bit older, they will prompt him to ask questions. The letters aren't dated, but they're numbered and David has included clues in each one which give an indication of when they were written.

"I've done that purposefully because I've wanted to create – not a mystery necessarily – but an environment where there are questions and therefore an opportunity for answers to come from parents and not necessarily me. I wanted to write stories that were not parables, but had that sense that they needed translation, interpretation."

A recurring theme in the letters is spirituality – a reflection of David's strong Christian beliefs.

"I read the *Bible* and therefore I have my own understanding of what is important in that area, so I wanted to say that too. In our western society we've lost a lot of understanding of spirituality and I think it's a tremendous shame because it's such an important part of life to be able to trust outside your own sphere and

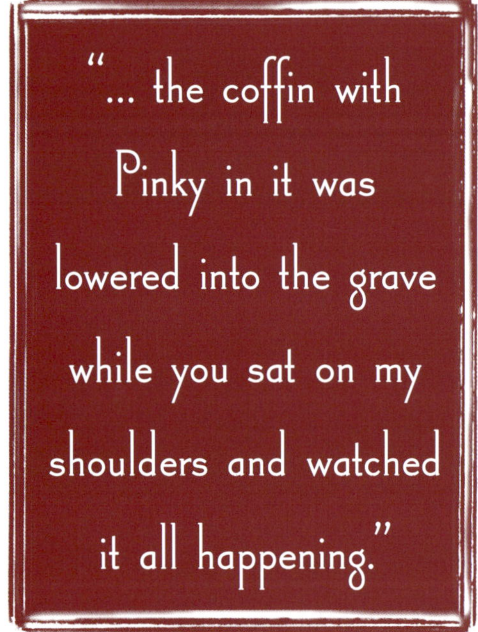

outside of what you even understand."

Rachel, David's daughter and Ihaka's mother, regards the letters as precious gifts.

"I thought it was wonderful. What I'm going to do eventually is put them all in a lovely, big book for him."

David says one reason for his concerted effort at being a good grandparent is that he missed out on a close relationship with his own grandparents.

"I really didn't know my grandparents. All I knew of my mother's father was that he was a tease. My father's father died because he was run over by a train."

"On the way to a prayer meeting!" interjects Rachel.

"Yes, on the way to a prayer meeting," smiles David. "So I thought I never found out anything about these people – not even a page."

David asked to be photographed with his computer because it has become a central part of his life; he travels the world, working with indigenous people and recording their spiritual music.

"I do a lot of travel around the Earth and I always take my computer and a printer with me – that's my office. Now a lot of my contemporaries wouldn't even do that sort of thing, but then I realise when Ihaka is turning 30 what I'm doing now will be so obsolete!"

1998 letter from David Garratt to his grandson Ihaka:

Birth & Death

Ihaka, two of the things we can be certain of are birth and death. We don't have anything at all to do with our birth – that's entirely to do with our mum and dad and we just arrive.

As far as death is concerned, we usually don't have much idea when that is going to come either.

These two very important events happen to us all, but one thing we do have a lot to do with are the years between them. Every day we live has its own value. We can encourage and help people around us, or we can make life miserable for them. Life has many choices.

Your dad's mother, who was named Whena (although you called her Pinky), died a couple of months back. She had been sick a long time and for the last weeks of her life she was in the hospital at Green lane.

I went up to see her a couple of times and she talked about looking forward to being with Jesus. She wanted to be free from the discomfort she felt for so long. She was finding breathing so difficult.

Although she was ready to die and wanted to, it was sad for Grandad and of course all of us.

After she died we had her tangi, firstly a service in Auckland and then up north, where she came from.

All the family sat together on blankets next to her body as she lay in the coffin. Lots of people talked about her, reminding each other of what she had done and how good she was. The people laughed and cried. It was a wonderful time. At one stage when we were up north at Te Kao your mother asked me to hold you. After a while you went off to sleep in my arms while all the speeches and songs were going on.

Then on the Sunday – Pinky died on the Thursday before – the coffin was closed and we all left the marae and went down to the little Anglican church for her final service. It was sad, but also a very proper ending to a wonderful life. Your father spoke so well, I was proud of him.

At the back of the church building were a lot of grave stones where people had been buried over the years.

The grave diggers in the town had dug a hole for Pinky's coffin. It was a work of art, made just the right size for her.

After a brief few words from the minister, the coffin with Pinky in it was lowered into the grave while you sat on my shoulders and watched it all happening. Then people came to the grave and dropped flowers and said their final goodbye. There were many tears.

In five weeks' time you are going to have a new sister. The story of birth and death…

Pat & Russell Tulloch & their great-granddaughter Tatiana

When Pat and Russell Tulloch first moved to Ruatahuna, deep in the heart of the Urewera, they planned to be there for around six weeks.

While Russell was "tickled pink" at the prospect of heading to a hunting and fishing paradise, Pat was concerned about the isolation. Ruatahuna is one of New Zealand's most isolated villages, separated by a hellish two-and-a-half-hour drive through dusty plains and dense bush.

Almost 50 years down the track, they're still there and proud of the fact that Ruatahuna will always be home for their seven surviving children, 19 grandchildren and now their young great-grandchild, Tatiana (pictured).

"I call it my Shangri-La," grins Russell, a retired builder, storekeeper and forestry worker (among other things). "It's at the head of the Whakatane River in a beautiful open valley and there's nothing to indicate that it's here until you pop around the corner and boofta! Here it is!"

You have to be somewhat committed to "pop around the corner". Whether travelling from Wairoa in the east, through Waikaremoana, or Rotorua in the west through the Kaingaroa Forest, you face a long, slow drive over a

notoriously difficult road which winds its way through dense, virgin bush before opening out to the Ruatahuna Valley.

But Russell and Pat reckon it's well worth the drive.

The first time they ever tackled it together was back in 1951 when Russell's eldest brother bought a business which included running the local school bus and store.

"The store was a bit Eb and Zeb [falling down]," says Russell. "The local authority were going to close him down if he didn't upgrade the facilities and, me being a carpenter and a bit of a handyman, he sent an SOS so my wife and I – we had only been married 12 months and were living in North Canterbury – trekked up to Ruatahuna – temporarily. I promised my wife it would be for six weeks – she didn't want to come here at all!"

But one thing led to another and before long Russell was flat out building houses for Maori, funded by the old Maori Affairs Department.

"I was attracted to the place straight away. There is marvellous hunting and fishing – you could throw your line in the river and catch a trout any time – and we had deer literally on our doorstep. When kids started coming that kept mother amused and she got to know local people. Maori people are very friendly and these people are exceptional folk, very hospitable.

"The Maori settlement goes way back – pre-European – and because of the rugged nature of the Urewera, the food resources were pretty skimpy compared to the coastal areas. They are a pretty hardy race," he says.

Asked how many Pakeha faces there are in Ruatahuna, Russell bursts into laughter. "Bugger all! There were a few Pakehas around when the mill was here. At the moment there's only the farm manager and the young fella who works for the Department of Conservation and myself. The wife doesn't qualify because she's part-Maori."

In those early days the occasional trips out of the area were a mission. "We had a little 1936 Austin, 10 horse power," he chuckles. "You always put two-and-a-half hours on a trip to Rotorua. That was the easiest way to go because, even though it was exactly halfway between Wairoa and Rotorua, the Wairoa end, through Waikaremoana, was half an hour longer. There were clouds of pumice dust in the summer time driving across the Kaingaroa Plains, but it was all relative."

After almost 10 years building houses, Russell took over the local store, run as a coopcrative, and built it up to a successful business until it burnt down under suspicious circumstances many years ago. Then it was a stint in the Forestry Service before retirement at 60.

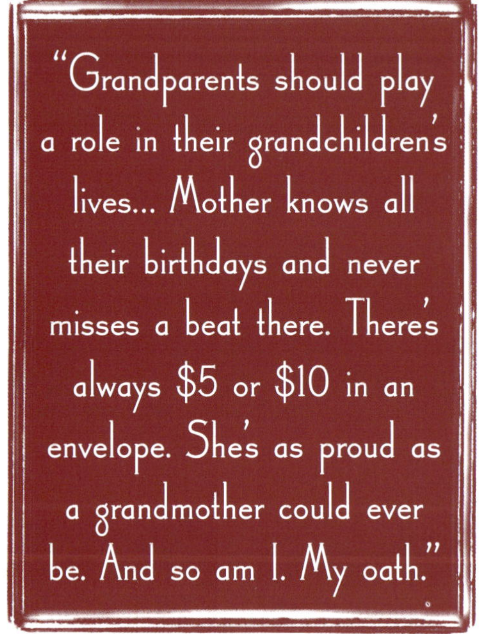

He and Pat had eight children, but their eldest son was killed in an accident at the mill at the age of seven.

It's a source of great pride to Russell that all their surviving children and grandchildren are "within spitting distance" of Ruatahuna – in Turangi, Rotorua, Whakatane, Murupara and Kaingaroa.

He says growing up in a Maori community has had a major influence on the family. "Maori values have rubbed off on our family. They are much more family-oriented than Pakehas are. Everybody is an uncle or an aunty and, as long as you have whanau and you can relate to a whakapapa [genealogy], you belong."

Many of the Tulloch children have paired up with Maori partners, and Russell says between all seven kids and their partners, "We have every Maori tribe represented!

"All the grandchildren have grown up like brothers and sisters rather than cousins."

He adores having the little ones around and Tatiana is his pride and joy. "She's a dag."

Pat agrees. "She's a good girl. She sings, she watches her videos and amuses herself – she's one of those kids. She loves the cat and just potters around. She's our first great-grandchild and her mother was our first grandchild, so that makes it special."

The couple like to spend as much time as possible with their grandchildren, but Russell admits his patience runs thin at times.

"Some of the ones in their teens get up my nose a bit. It's the old story: you expect the standards of behaviour that applied to us oldies when we were their age. They seem to get away with a hell of a lot more. The materialism is something I'm not quite used to, where they get everything. Their attention spans leave a lot to be desired and I put that down to the consumer society."

Like so many of his generation, Russell grew up knowing how to make his own fun and keep himself amused, so he's not impressed with kids who cry "boredom" when they're out in the countryside. "I'm never backward in coming forward in tuning them up when it's necessary. I always do it with good humour and my tongue in my cheek. They reckon I'm a grumpy, old bugger.

"I just don't like dudes hanging about with their ears flapping when adults are talking… or boys with their hands in their pocket. I say, 'Get the hell on out of here; get down the creek.' They say, 'Oh we have nothing to do'. I say, 'Build a hut!' Those are the kinds of things I get impatient with because, when I was a kid, the days were never long enough. I was never at home. There was always the river."

But then he grins again. "They'll probably be saying the same thing when their grandchildren are around."

Russell hasn't the strength he once had to take the kids fishing and hunting because he has emphysema, a chronic lung disease. But he still believes he can play an important role in their lives – what's more it's his responsibility.

"Grandparents should play a role in their grandchildren's lives, and if they don't they bloody well should. Mother knows all their birthdays and never misses a beat there. There's always $5 or $10 in an envelope. She's as proud as a grandmother could ever be. And so am I. My oath."

Jack Lowe & his granddaughter Junaye-Maree

Sitting on his father's grave, with his granddaughter on his knee, Jack Lowe takes a quiet moment to reflect on memories of his father, Cum Choen Lowe.

This may be three-year-old Junaye-Maree's earliest memory of an ancient practice dating back generations in the Lowe family history. Twice a year, in April and October, Jack and his extended family of around 30 people meet at Auckland's Purewa Cemetery laden with fish, chicken, rice, fruit, cake, wine and tea to pay tribute to their ancestors.

The October visit is based on the Chung Yang Chieh [The Double Ninth] Festival and is based on the belief that the well-being of one's ancestors will ensure the family's prosperity, health and blessings.

Jack, a retired market gardener and fruiterer of Mt Roskill who has lived in New Zealand for 40 years, has strictly observed both festivals for as long as he can remember. Five of his relatives are buried at Purewa: his father, mother, father-in-law, first wife and brother.

A strict protocol is observed during the festival. The graves must be visited in order of seniority – eldest ancestors first. Family members offer prayers at each site, bowing three times to show respect – the number three is important in Chinese culture and represents Heaven, Earth and Man. They then burn incense and money and spill rice wine and tea around the grave, offering food before moving to the next site. When all the graves have been visited, the group returns to the resting place of the most senior ancestor, in this case Jack's father, and have their picnic.

It's an ideal opportunity for the whole family to gather to catch up with each other. "For the older generations it's one of the reasons they go, to see all the family members."

Ancient customs are preserved, such as offering only foods that have a head and a tail – the fruit as well as the fish and chicken are served whole. "That's because everything has a beginning and an end," explains Jack.

Sadly for him, the tradition may come to an end in the Lowe family when he dies. "It's really only for the old people – I think the magic is there because they really believe in it. The drive comes from that generation so when they're gone I don't think it will continue."

Diggeress Te Kanawa & her granddaughter Clowdy

Tears are welling up again in Clowdy Te Kanawa's eyes as she sits at her grandmother's feet and explains why she's feeling so miserable.

Ten days ago the 22-year-old moved out of the cottage next door to her grandparents' Oparure home. She's now just 10 minutes' drive away in Te Kuiti, but is feeling desperately homesick. "I haven't stopped crying for the last week and a half. I've been a real crying little girl," she says, smiling despite herself.

This is not the first time Clowdy has moved away from her grandparents' house, but it is the first time she has left their shelter since overcoming a battle with alcohol and drug addiction.

"Since I've been sober over the last five years it's like I've come home again and never actually left home. Nan and Poppa mean that much to me," she muses. "But crying is not a bad thing. It's a way of measuring my happiness and I must have been really happy with them to cry for a week and a half."

While Clowdy speaks, her grandmother, eminent Maori weaver Diggeress Te Kanawa, sits quietly on the sofa while her grandfather Tangitehau (Tana) lounges in his chair in the corner, reading the paper and pouring a fresh cup of tea every now and again. It's a relaxed, quiet, secure place and it's easy to see why she would hate to leave.

"Nan and Poppa are my poutokomanawa, my centre pole really. People will go through trials and tribulations in life and if they don't have something that's really stable they often can veer off the track, but I've always had something really stable in my life."

That stability was critical during Clowdy's childhood. With her parents estranged, the responsibility for raising her swung between her mother, her grandparents and, for a while, her father. The happiest times of her childhood were the first eight years she spent under her grandparents' roof.

"I remember when I was really young my mum used to live here with me and I used to go to sleep with my mum and wake up between Nana and Poppa," says Clowdy. "When I was older Mum told me that Nan used to say to Poppa, 'go and get that girl', and Mum used to be lying there and he'd come in and steal me out of bed and I'd wake up in their bed. By the time I was five I used to just get up and go and lie there myself."

But then Clowdy's mother embarked on a new course of education and took Clowdy with her while she studied in Wellington and then Canberrra, Australia. "When she did that she took me away from Nana and Poppa, which was the first time I had been away from them."

The experience was devastating for Digger. "That broke my heart," she says simply. "I didn't like her going to Australia so I thought, 'We'll keep an eye on her from afar' and she might come back and that's what she did."

But by then, Clowdy was a troubled young woman, clashing badly with her mother and already experimenting with drugs and alcohol.

"When she came back from Australia she was a bit lost, but I think it was like coming home to a bit of warmth and so we just coasted along."

Not long after returning, Clowdy moved out again, this time to live with her father in Te Kuiti, a man she had had little to do with in her life so far. "At that stage my father drove a Harley Davidson and was oh so very cool so I went to live with him and my step-mother."

Clowdy's own crisis came when she fell seriously ill – a combination of stress and substance abuse. She was told she would have to go to hospital. Instead, she called her mother and asked to be taken around to her grandparents' house.

"That's where I got better," she says.

It wasn't an easy road. She was suffering a severe kidney infection, was undernourished, exhausted and even hallucinating. Her desperately worried grandparents nursed her through it all.

"I suppose that was the time I realised how close my grandmother was to me because she tangied for me while I was sick," says Clowdy. "She cried for me. I knew that she could feel my pain. She cried for me and I suppose that's where I realised how important it was to have a family that is really close and love that is unconditional. I had been away for all that time and I had put my grandparents through a lot of stuff because I was very manipulative."

Digger doesn't like to look back on those days. "The problem was I think she was torn between her mother and father," she says, adding that Clowdy's parents had problems of their own. "There was a lot of turmoil in her life, but when it got a bit heavy she would come back."

Relative to those times, the last five years have been smooth sailing as Clowdy gradually recovered and turned her efforts towards helping others, recently graduating as a drug and alcohol counsellor herself.

"I didn't like it at all when she started that," admits Digger. "She is so young. When she used to get back at the end of the day she was very quiet and looked tired and said she had a very heavy day. I would say a little prayer to myself and hope it would be okay because I couldn't imagine what it's like to counsel people like that because you never came across that sort of problem in our day."

On the other hand, Digger is proud of her granddaughter's commitment to helping others. "She seems strong. She has turned out a very strong person and she's kind of there for anyone in the family who needs her. I have another grandson who is just coming out of rehabilitation for alcohol and drugs in Auckland and I feel so hopeless. When I wanted to talk to him and get him to pull himself together Clowdy said, 'That's the last thing you do. It's a waste of time. They have to decide it themselves before something can be done.' So you see I'm still learning."

Clowdy acknowledges she still leans on her grandparents when it all gets too much. "This is my nurturing place. I work with something that is very confusing. It is important for me to have somewhere that is grounded, that is really stable.

"There are certain morals and values that I think you get from your grandparents; things like whanau, family and how important that is and how important it is to support one another. They are very, very simple principles in life that are often overlooked now. They are things about being good to one another and looking after one another."

Clowdy's motives for moving away from her grandparents were partly driven by a sense of fairness towards other members of the family who haven't had the opportunity to get as close as she has to her grandparents. Both Digger and Tana are in fragile health and Clowdy knows their time is limited.

"Because Nan and Poppa are getting older, I think I can move away so other people can have a chance to be with them. It's not going to be that long and I think it would be easier for people to come and look after them without me being here. It's about giving other people a turn at having that relationship with them."

But Clowdy will still be a regular visitor – especially if she

is to fulfil her dream of becoming an accomplished weaver like her grandmother and great-grandmother, the esteemed Rangimarie Hetet – both considered among the greatest weavers of their generations.

For more years than she likes to remember, Digger has been working on making a korowai or feather cloak for each of her 12 children. Although she's now working on the 11th, none of her children have any idea which korowai is destined for which person, because she's keeping it a mystery until all 12 are complete.

Digger is delighted that Clowdy recently expressed her desire to learn to weave, but there hasn't been much time to teach her because the young woman has been so busy with her work and studies. "We haven't got much time together so she sees me teaching others and gets a bit envious!"

What Clowdy hasn't yet told her grandmother is the reason she wants to learn to weave is to make her grandmother the ultimate gift: a korowai of her own.

"I know she's never been given one," says Clowdy. "She's given and given and given, but she's never been given one and for me it's about time I made one. That would be the ultimate way to honour her journey with me. I know Nan and Poppa are getting older and she's not 100 per cent well. I just hope that time is on my side."

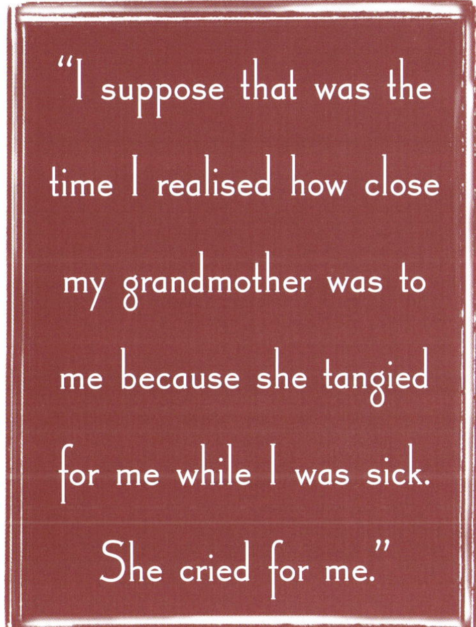

Mary Williams
& her
granddaughter Johanna

The first wedding among the grandchildren is always a special one, but Mary Williams, 72, was particularly chuffed when she learned her granddaughter Johanna was to marry.

Johanna, 23, and her husband, Hendrik Wassenaar, wanted to involve family members as much as possible on their New Zealand wedding day (they also had a ceremony in Hendrik's home country, Holland) so asked Mary whether she would consider doing a Bible reading for their ceremony.

"It was very important to me that she was there," says Johanna. "I would not have done it without her."

Mary was delighted at the request. "I was quite excited about her getting married and particularly excited when she asked me to participate. I thought that was lovely."

Sir Paul Reeves & his granddaughter Roimata

Sir Paul Reeves sits quietly in his downtown Auckland office, his eyes scrutinising a photograph of his granddaughter playing with him in a tent.

At the ripe old age of six, the child is clearly at home in her skin: self-assured, a little mischievous and full of anticipation of fun-filled adventures ahead.

There was a time when Sir Paul, as a boy, had the same sort of confidence. But that was before he started school in the working class and predominantly white Wellington suburb of Newtown and realised the skin he had felt so comfortable in was actually a problem.

"Darkie" was the term they used in the schoolyard in those days and the boy came to hear it so much that he began to turn away from a heritage he blamed for making him the target of those taunts.

"I didn't know what to do with that description," he says. "It differentiated me from everybody else and I had no cultural or human equipment to deal with this factor that other people were identifying in me. So you end up by denying who you are. Denying that my mother and grandmother were Maori was the easiest way out."

This may be one reason why he falls silent when he examines the photograph of Roimata with her chocolate brown eyes, corkscrew hair and skin the colour of manuka honey.

"Her name is Roimata. Her skin is brown," he muses. "I hope that in a suburb like Ponsonby and in a city like Auckland in Aotearoa today that she won't have to deal with those sorts of things. Rather there can be a positive enhancement and recognition of – without being too crass – the fact that brown is beautiful."

He doesn't say it, but perhaps now he is a grandparent, he can sense the confusion his own grandmother would have felt had she known of his struggle with their shared culture.

Sir Paul put those schoolyard experiences behind him long ago, and feels secure as a Maori. In fact, these days he sees one of the most important roles he and Roimata's other grandfather can play in her life as being to help her

find a place for herself within Maori culture.

"One of the things grandparents can do is to be the transmitter of memories and culture," he explains. "Carefully you try to locate the kids within the generations that precede them and maybe the generations that follow them. It is important to give grandchildren the sense they are part of a continuous stream of history and humanity bound together by common inheritance and bloodlines. They need a sense that they have received the heritage from the past as a gift. Their job is to make sure that they take care of this gift and to hand it on to succeeding generations."

It may sound like a heavy weight, but the reality is filled with humour and affection as the photographs come out and Sir Paul tells stories about his mother and grandmother, whose portraits come to life before Roimata's eyes.

This transfer of memories and culture is particularly important in Maori culture says Sir Paul. "Traditionally you would find that often a grandchild would be fostered by the grandparents – not for the purpose of cutting off links with the parents or because the parents were necessarily not being good parents – but rather to give the child the chance to be in this nest, this repository where memories and history and stories can be transmitted and where they can feel the warmth of a wider family relationship."

For the first few years of Roimata's life, there wasn't much opportunity for Sir Paul to transmit much to her because while she was living in Rarotonga, he was jetsetting between the United States, New Zealand and more recently Fiji. However, now that the whole family is settled back in Auckland, Sir Paul, the former Anglican Archbishop and Governor-General, is delighting in the opportunity to get to know his granddaughter and her younger brother, Ben, aged three.

"Well she's coming up seven now," he says. "She draws like crazy. Our fridge door is covered with her paintings and she has a nice sense of colour and form. So to draw and to read seem to be things that she wants to do. There's an inquiring mind there and expressive ability.

"She has the normal range of human emotions that kids have, ranging from a smile through to a pout and sometimes a tear or two. That's pretty normal," he smiles, acknowledging that adjustments have to be made when you have children around the house – such as getting used to mess and clutter.

"That can be difficult because older people do place a

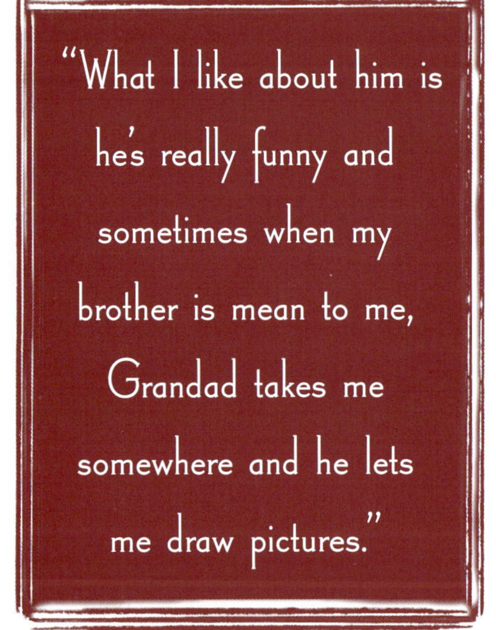

store by order or dependability and predictability. Younger kids don't know much about that stuff so if they are going to make a mess then what we do is let them make a mess, but confine it a bit. We say to them: 'you're over there and you're not over here,'" he laughs.

The term "older people" rolls off his tongue and Roimata does sometimes make him feel his age. "I do note with some wistfulness that our children attend weddings and baptisms and I attend funerals."

But he's not complaining. "I feel young at heart and I don't feel I have to resist the obvious fact that I'm getting older. It would be stupid to deny that and yet I don't give in to any people's presuppositions of what people of my age should do. I think I can go out and find that out for myself, having been to the gym this morning for instance," he grins.

"Does Roimata see me as old? I don't know how she sees me, probably as part of the furniture, part of the background, someone whose home she visits every now and then. I'm part of the — in my words — loving network."

Well yes, Roimata does confess to regarding her Grandad as "a little old". But she's quick to add that he's "a little younger too" because she's seen photos of him as a young man with her mum, Sarah.

"I call him Grandad," she says. "What I like about him is he's really funny and sometimes when my brother is mean to me, Grandad takes me somewhere and he lets me draw pictures."

For Roimata, the times spent with her grandfather revolve around drawing, playing cricket or catch or listening to Sir Paul's wonderful stories. "He tells me stories about Harry the Helicopter. He thinks of them and then I come over and sleep and he tells me them. Some of them are scary and some of them are fun."

Roimata is well aware of her grandfather's high profile. "Sometimes he's on the TV and we see him and we ring him up to tell him he's on TV! One time we saw him at a meeting with Jenny Shipley!"

And what would Sir Paul like Roimata to remember about him when he is gone? "I would like her to have the memory of someone who was good to be around, who read books and had ideas and responded to the stimulus of the natural and human environment. I would like her to know that he loved her and loved her parents and after that you start making religious statements!"

Sir Paul notes with some pleasure that Roimata and her family go to church. "We're pleased with that although when she came home very proud on Good Friday and said: 'Grandad, I banged in a nail!' I thought: 'Oh God!'" He laughs again. "I will be pretty relaxed in her attitude toward religion. Yes, I like people to go to church but I feel that, at the end of the day, what I measure as the signs of religion in people is something to do with a quality they basically have."

Meanwhile Sir Paul's hopes for Roimata's future are quite simple. "All I can say is that Roimata's parents have achieved because of their ability and that if Roimata has ability then I will be working very hard and I'm sure her parents will for that ability to find its role and place in society. I hope that whatever she does with her abilities will be for her own development as a person and also, in some way, for the betterment and the richness of the community and society around her."

Sara Ammali & her grandparents Nada & Mile Ivanovic

Little Sara Ammali hasn't seen much of her grandparents since emigrating from Serbia to New Zealand in 1996.

But her Serbian grandparents "Baba" [Grandma] Nada and "Deda" [Grandpa] Mile Ivanovic made up for lost time on their first trip out to see their only granddaughter.

Mile set about building Sara her own little playhouse while Nada took care of the colour scheme: painting it sky blue with little white daisies.

"My dad enjoys working with wood so he decided to make a wooden house when he was out here," says Sara's mother, Snezana Ivanovic-Ammali. "It is so sweet – it looks like something out of Hansel and Gretel. My parents spent a lot of time with Sara in that house."

It became clear during their six-month visit that Snezana's parents missed their only granddaughter dreadfully. "I think she is special to them because she's a girl," says Snezana. "I think my dad always wanted to have boys because he only had two daughters but as soon as he got male grandsons he realised what a pleasure girls are! Sara will just sit and they can talk to her and they just enjoy that time. The house was a place they would go for stories: they would sit inside there making up stories, reading or colouring in."

While Sara already speaks excellent English her mother insists she keep up her Serbian language skills – mostly for her grandparents' sake. "My parents would be very, very upset if they couldn't have a conversation with her!"

In Serbia, grandparents traditionally play a significant role in the lives of their grandchildren and Snezana does feel Sara is missing out being so far away from her grandparents. "What we say is that when you are a parent you don't have much time for the kids so you miss some things – but their grandparents are retired and have more time to develop a relationship with the kids."

However she and her husband, Brahim Ammali, an Algerian, were prepared to make that sacrifice when they emigrated to New Zealand in 1996, partly for economic reasons, partly because of the political strife that for the last decade has plagued the region formerly known as Yugoslavia.

"There are a whole lot of issues that forced us to leave our country and come over here," explains Snezana. "We didn't feel like we wanted to raise our daughter in that atmosphere. It was a very hard decision and was selfish from my parents' point of view but we also felt that we are responsible for us and Sara too and that's why we came to New Zealand."

Snezana and Brahim never discuss the conflicts in the former Yugoslavia with the child. "We just try to avoid all the bad things and politics is not for kids anyway," says Snezana. "I just share my language, my stories, my songs and lots of love."

Snezana is confident Mile and Nada will continue to make extended visits to New Zealand to spend six months at a time with their granddaughter.

"There is a saying in Serbia that if you are young you like to escape your parents but as soon as you have children of your own you like to be close to them!" she laughs. "Well that's how it goes. We really love New Zealand and enjoy living here. Our only regret in coming here is that Sara is not with her grandparents."

> "We just try to avoid all the bad things and politics is not for kids anyway... I just share my language, my stories, my songs and lots of love."